Turning Pages

Turning Pages

The Adventures and Misadventures of a Publisher

John Sargent

Arcade Publishing · New York

Arcade Publishing books may be purchased in bulk at special discounts for sales promotion, corporate gifts, fund-raising, or educational purposes. Special editions can also be created to specifications. For details, contact the Special Sales Department, Arcade Publishing, 307 West 36th Street, 11th Floor, New York, NY 10018 or arcade@skyhorsepublishing.com.

Arcade Publishing® is a registered trademark of Skyhorse Publishing, Inc.®, a Delaware corporation.

Visit our website at www.arcadepub.com.

10 9 8 7 6 5 4 3 2 1

Library of Congress Cataloging-in-Publication Data is available on file.

Cover design by David Ter-Avanesyan

Print ISBN: 978-1-956763-85-0
Ebook ISBN: 978-1-956763-86-7

Printed in the United States of America

For Connie, Kyle, and Jack, with love.

Contents

PART IV: FINAL CHAPTER

Author's Note

THIS BOOK IS MOSTLY ABOUT MY LIFE AT WORK. I WROTE IT EPI-sodically to let the best stories of my publishing career speak for themselves. The events described are my memory of what transpired; other people may recall things differently. Where possible, I have fact-checked the stories with the people involved to ensure accuracy. I have used quotes to record the exact words of written documents, but also to describe conversations as best as I can recall them. I have tried not to offend, and I apologize if I have. Many of the people I cherish the most do not appear in these pages; there is a sort of tyranny to telling only the good stories.

Prologue

I AM A LOW-HANGING BRANCH ON TWO NOTABLE FAMILY TREES. On my dad's side there was a famous early feminist, an important conservationist who helped save America's forests, an artist of stellar reputation, and a doctor who took a bullet in the J. P. Morgan assassination attempt. Mom's side was less varied. There was a general who fired the first shot in the Civil War and a whole bunch of book people. The book people go back three generations and include, among others, five authors, three chief executives of publishing companies, one independent bookstore owner, and an editor-in-chief. Throw in my generation, add the book people on the Sargent side, and you get another two chief executives, two more authors, two more independent bookstore owners, another editor-in-chief, and a guy who ran book clubs. The family accounted for a lot of ink.

My mother's grandfather, Frank Nelson Doubleday, was born in 1862 and grew up in Brooklyn, sixteen blocks and a world away from where I live today. He started his first business at age eleven, printing advertising flyers on a hand-cranked single-sheet press in his basement. At age fourteen, when his father's hat business failed, he quit school and went to work for Charles Scribner, a prominent publisher of the time. Frank did well, and in his late twenties, he came up with an interesting idea. Frank took a train to Vermont to pitch his idea to a popular author of the day. The plan was to publish the author's previous books in a handsome series; never mind that the books were owned by other publishers. The notable author liked young Doubleday's plan, and Frank set to work. It was a daunting task, but he finally convinced the publishers to cooperate, and the series was a huge success. The author, Rudyard Kipling, would become a central figure in Frank's life, and years later would give him the nickname "Effendi" (Turkish for chief, and a play on his initials FND). Frank would no longer be called Frank; he was Effendi from that point forward.

In 1897, at the age of thirty-five, Effendi started his own publishing company with a partner. Kipling joined on, and the company's first major bestseller was *Captains Courageous*. Then, in the company's second year, Joseph Conrad provided *Lord Jim*. Effendi's wife, Neltje, also took pen in hand. She was a scientific historian who wrote eleven bestselling books about birds and flowers under the pen name of Neltje Blanchan. Family lore suggests she did it to keep the company presses running in a tough time; I have always suspected it had more to do with expressing her remarkable talent. At the age of fifty-two, while in China on a special mission for the Red Cross, Neltje contracted a rare virus. She never made it home. She left behind four children, two of whom worked at Doubleday. Nelson, her eldest child, would show great promise and early on would take over his mother's role generating sales for the company.

When Nelson was a schoolboy, he came to his father with a book proposal. He had just read a short story written by his Uncle Rud, about how a leopard got its spots. Nelson's concept was a book about how animals got their seemingly strange features; his example was how an elephant got its trunk. Effendi suggested he write Uncle Rud with his idea. Always sharp, the kid asked what would be in it for him if the book got published. Effendi promised a one penny royalty, I imagine with a chuckle. Nelson would get a one penny royalty for the rest of his life on every copy sold of *The Just So Stories*.

By the time he died, Effendi had built Doubleday into the largest book publisher in America. Nelson took over from his father. He accelerated the growth of the publishing operation and turned a secondhand magazine business that he started in high school into the largest direct-mail book club company in the United States. He was a hands-on publisher. In the late 1930s, he worried about the safety of one of his favorite authors, Somerset Maugham. Sensing the coming war and fearing his friend would have nowhere to live, Nelson built him a writer's cottage behind his house. Maugham wrote *A Razor's Edge* in that cottage, and I wrote much of this manuscript on Maugham's old desk.

Nelson and his wife Ellen had a son they named Nelson Jr. The senior Nelson, at six-foot-seven, naturally became known as Big Nelson in the family. Then they had a daughter who they named Neltje, in honor of her grandmother. Big Nelson died young in 1949, when Neltje, my mother, was only fourteen. After his death, Ellen fought fiercely to keep the company private and family owned. Her intent was to pass it on to her son, Nelson Jr.

My father, John Sargent, started at Doubleday in 1946. He was an up-and-coming executive when, at the age of twenty-eight, he married Neltje, the boss's daughter. She was eighteen. Dad made it to the top and ran the company for fifteen years with great success. And he had some fun along the way: how many people can say Theodore Roethke regularly slept in their bathtub? The peak of my father's publishing career came in the mid-1970s, when Doubleday published *Jaws* and *Roots* in a two-year span.

In 1978, when Ellen died, my uncle Nelson (called, a bit cruelly, Little Nelson) took control of the ownership of Doubleday. Like his father before him, Nelson Jr. had worked in the company his entire career. When he gained control, he promptly pushed my father into the chairman's role. Eight years later, in 1986, Nelson sold the company to Bertelsmann. By then it was a media conglomerate in books, bookstores, book clubs, textbooks, printing, radio, sports, and, for one movie (A *Parallax View* starring Warren Beatty), the movies. But before the sale went through, Nelson spun off a single asset from the company, the New York Mets. Doubleday had purchased the team six years before for a paltry twenty-one million dollars, and now Nelson took over ownership personally. He walked away from the book business he had inherited. Fair enough. Nelson always loved baseball, and he loved that a Doubleday had supposedly invented it; books were a family passion, but they were not his passion.

For three generations, Doubleday the business was highly successful. Doubleday the family was less so. A focus on the company, and an appetite for booze, often led to frayed relationships. By all reports, my grandfather was estranged from his sister. In the next generation, my mother was not on speaking terms with her brother for most of her adult life. They had different views of the world, they rarely respected each other's decisions, and my mother always resented Nelson's control of the company. She felt he had earned that control by being born male, and she was right. Their relationship fell apart over money, failed trust, and extremely bad behavior. At one point, feeling there was no other solution, my mother sued her brother, her mother, and my father over company ownership issues. She lost. Then she appealed. And she lost again. Meanwhile, when Nelson sold the company, he didn't bother to tell her. This sort of thing can make family gatherings a bit stressful.

When I was six, my mom and dad separated. When I was eight, they divorced. My father stayed at the company in New York, while my mother moved from her Park Avenue apartment to a small cattle ranch twenty miles southeast of Sheridan, Wyoming. Trading in square feet for acreage, she planned to start a completely new life. She was done with the family, with the publishing business, with fancy people, fancy parties, and with her husband who she married too quickly. Instead, she would be a rancher and an artist. She took her kids along for the ride.

I grew up working on the ranch. When I was in fourth and fifth grade, my older sister Ellen and I went to a one-room schoolhouse eight miles away in Ucross, population twelve. Our teacher picked us up every morning on her drive out from Sheridan; we were two of eleven kids randomly scattered from first to eighth grade. Ellen had Sandy Seymour in her class, and I had Bo Smith in mine. There were plenty of cows around, but not enough children. The next year they closed the school.

We transferred to Woodland Park in town, a school mostly for ranch kids from all over southern Sheridan County. The bus ride was an hour and a half in and two hours home; Woodland Park was nothing like the last full-sized school I had attended, the Dalton School in Manhattan. Before we got on the bus at 7:00 a.m., I had an hour of chores. When we got home, I had two hours more. At school disagreements were settled with fists, and the teachers were armed with paddles they knew how to use. There was a toughness in the place, but there was plenty of small-town kindness as well. At home, Ellen and I weathered adolescence, a difficult stepfather, and our complicated mother.

We led mostly a ranch life, but every summer, after the hay was bailed and stacked, Ellen and I would fly alone back to the East Coast. This required a shifting of gears. Being a small part of our father's bachelor-fueled A-list social life was . . . different. A sort of parallel universe with Dad's endless string of girlfriends, no chores, and a beach house. There were nannies, fancy restaurants, celebrities, and movies you could see on first release. Hard to explain to the kids back home.

I went to Sheridan High School as a freshman before attending a progressive boarding school of small repute. I called home once a month, but Ellen's letters and chocolate chip cookies arrived regularly. I went to college in California. I can still remember the joy I felt driving down the back side of the Sierra Nevada, windows down, the Detroit Spinners turned up.

I had a good time in college. My transcript was decent enough, but there was a recession in 1979 and I struggled to get a job. I needed a next step, so with some hesitation, I signed up for a publishing course. Though I had no burning desire to be a publisher, I thought I would see what the family business was all about. From the course, I got a job as a textbook salesman. Nobody ever dreams of being a textbook salesman. During the next two years, some people discovered who my father was, but nobody knew about the Doubleday side of my family. I would try to keep it that way.

I went from the sales job to business school and from business school to a job in the back office of Doubleday in Garden City, Long Island. I got married. Four years later I left Doubleday, and a guy named Jeremiah Kaplan gave me my big break; Jerry had faith in me when others didn't. He took a risk and hired me at Checkerboard Press, and then, less than two years later, he took another risk and hired me at Simon & Schuster. I would work at S&S, running the Children's Book Division, for six years. I lasted longer than Jerry. I had two children, five years apart, a daughter named Kyle and a son named Jack. We chose to give them their own names, free of ancestral heritage. After S&S, I ran the US operation of Dorling Kindersley for three years. Then I joined St. Martin's Press, Holtzbrinck Publishers, and Macmillan, where I ran things for twenty-four years.

People who knew my family history would always say that I had publishing in my blood. It never felt that way to me. But for all I know, Effendi's genes helped me with my publishing decisions, and if they did, I'm forever grateful. I know I was lucky to become a book publisher, and lots of that luck came from my family. If there was a starting point in who I became, though, it wasn't in my publishing roots. It was in the move westward and a summer spent on a sheep ranch in Wyoming's vast Powder River basin, where the rivers flow north.

PART I
Going West

Never turn off the ranch light. In the absolute dark, and in winter's drifting snow, the light will guide you home, and it will guide others in need of help or shelter.

1964–1974

I.

First Rodeo

THE AIR SEEMED ELECTRIC, SHARPENED BY MY FEAR. IT SMELLED of dirt, animals, and leather. I climbed down into the bucking chute and onto the back of what had been described as a large calf. It was clearly a small bull. My legs stretched outward, and it hurt to move my boots forward. As instructed, I put my right hand between the so-called calf's shoulders, palm up. A cowboy looped the rope over my leather glove and pulled it tight. So tight that when I tried to yank my hand free, it didn't budge. The calf banged against the iron chute; I could feel its muscles strain. I looked up at the cowboy and said, "Please, please, I don't want to do this."

He smiled down at me—"Sorry kid, too late"—and threw open the chute.

Welcome to the Little Levi Rodeo in Gillette, a small coal town in northeastern Wyoming. We had come looking for some Friday night excitement; we hadn't been off the TY ranch in what seemed like forever. We were staying with the Gibbs family; Martha Gibbs was my mother's roommate from boarding school. Martha had done that most romantic of things—she married a cowboy named Bobby. Now they owned the arid TY ranch, out on the Powder River, herding sheep for a living and raising four kids. We were camping out for six weeks in the Gibbs's yard, in a Winnebago. We had driven from New York City: my mother Neltje, her boyfriend John Kings, my sister Ellen, the son of one of Mom's friends named Kipper, the family dog, and me. It was fourteen miles of dirt road from the TY to the town of Arvada, a scant gathering of houses clustered around a bar. Take a left at Arvada and it was sixty empty miles to the Gillette fairgrounds and the bucking chutes.

When the chute opened, there was a moment of complete stillness. The sky was black. The vast expanse of arena dirt was dark and featureless. Between the two was a bank of glaring lights, the grandstand just a shadow behind them. Then suddenly I was face down in the dirt, unable to breathe, with the sharp pain of hooves on my back. A cowboy came, dragged me back to the chutes by the armpits, and propped me against the fence. He took off my borrowed spurs; the next kid needed them. In the shame of my tears, I sat alone, my legs stretched before me, my chin on my chest. I would get bucked off a lot in the years ahead, but at age seven this one would stick with me.

2.

Parental Moments

Mom

A year after our summer visit at the TY ranch, my mother pulled up stakes and left New York City. Always striving for the unexpected, she moved us to a ranch twenty miles outside of Sheridan, Wyoming, and a scant fifty miles from the Gibbs's place. Life suddenly featured cattle, unheard-of amounts of work, party line telephones, and no television.

Mom's unexpected moments, small and large, continued. There were little things, like never quite knowing what was going to be in your lunchbox. The nine other kids at our school marveled when our lunch turned out to be bologna and jelly sandwiches. Other small moments had longer-term impact. One fall afternoon, Ellen and I stood before Neltje at the washing machine. Her message was straightforward: "I'm not washing your sheets. You can wash them yourselves or I'll buy you sleeping bags." It was good news for me; I got to bed down in a flannel sleeping bag for the next six years. And to this day, I can still happily sleep without a pillow.

There were also larger unexpected moments. On an August afternoon, Mom married her boyfriend, John Kings, at the ranch. No warning was given. Ellen and I found out as we arrived home from an overnight visit to the TY ranch. When I asked why there were so many cars parked in the driveway, Martha Gibbs turned to us in the back seat, her eyes wide and startled. "Didn't your mother tell you?"

Some years later, when I was starting high school, Mom divorced John Kings. She piled everything he owned into his pickup and parked it at the grocery store in town. She called him to say, "Your stuff is in your truck at Safeway, never darken my door again." Then, a few weeks later, we had another direct conversation, this time in the kitchen. She told me she was legally changing her name. From now on she would be Neltje. She explained that she didn't like her father much, that my own father was an asshole, and that my stepfather was an even bigger asshole. She was done with being identified by the men in her life. From then on, my mother, like Cher before her, had only one name.

Dad

Late in high school, during one of my visits east, my father and I played a surprise game of golf. Dad stepped up to the ball at the first tee and did the little golfer's waggle. I thought, hey, maybe he is pretty good. Then he backed away, looked up the fairway, and addressed the ball for a second time. He paused. "I don't know if I should hit this ball or not." I asked him why and he replied, "Until I hit this ball, I can say the last time I played golf was with President Eisenhower." With that he hit the ball, a good shot, and the silence between us took its usual place. It was the last I heard of Ike.

Anthony

The memory stays clear, untouched by age. It is a warm day, in the stretched light of afternoon. I am on my bed, not yet fifteen, reading a book about my favorite topic, World War II. The book is about the Normandy invasion; the chapter is about the landing at one of the British beaches. The single paragraph is about a nineteen-year-old soldier named Anthony Rubinstein. It goes like this: The landing craft approached the beach, the front ramp dropped into waist deep water. The soldiers pushed forward. Rubenstein's best friend, directly in front of him, was shot in the head. The men rushed to the sand. The beach was horrific, the infantry pinned down by enemy fire. All the officers and many of the men were killed or wounded. Rubinstein took charge of those who were left, and by the end of the afternoon, the beachhead was secure.

I am amazed by the story. It seems so odd that this kid in the war had the same name as my mom's English boyfriend, who is sitting at the kitchen table downstairs. I start to do the math in my head. Oh my God, could it be? I run down the stairs and jump from the landing.

"Anthony, were you in World War II?"

He looks up, a bit startled, and says, "Yes, I was."

"Were you at D-Day?"

A strange thing happens then. His face, always so animated, goes still. His eyes seem to lose focus. He quietly says "Yes." I don't know what to do or say, but in his continued silence I realize the conversation is over. I go back upstairs, convinced now that I am living with that boy from the Normandy beach.

When my mom let Anthony go a few years later, it hurt. Unlike my stepfather before him, my sister and I adored "The Nose," a name he earned from a large proboscis and a great sense of humor. As the years passed, Anthony moved back to England, married, and lived happily. But he stayed in touch, and he stayed interested in us. He always took our side when we needed someone to; he was always caring. Over the years we would occasionally get together, mostly in New York.

The last time I saw Anthony, he took my wife Connie and me to the River Café in Brooklyn. Over dinner we enjoyed the view of Manhattan and the shimmering reflection of the Christmas lights. We told old stories, and I basked in his warmth. At some point, I asked him about his day, and he told us he had gone to church. "Church, not temple?" I asked.

He replied, "Not temple. Once a year I go to church, usually around Christmas." He said it softly, and then he told us why.

"I don't think I ever told you, but I fought in World War II. My best friend and I lied about our age and signed up before we turned eighteen. My first action was on D-Day. The landings were tough, my friend was killed, shot in the face before my eyes. I was stuck on the beach in a shallow trench for a long time; it was incredibly loud, the bullets very close. There was nothing to do but lie there and wait. A Bible was standard issue in our packs, and as the day wore on, I got it out and read. It made me feel better. Ever since, once a year, I go to church." It was clear, as it had been the first time all those years ago, that he was done talking about it. Our conversation moved on, and we parted that night with his usual bear hug.

I was crushed when Anthony died the next year. I thought of him often, and of that Normandy beach. I'll never know what happened; the recorded histories of the day are unclear. But this much I have discovered: Anthony Rubinstein was in B Troop of the Royal Marine Commandos. He landed on Juno Beach on June 6, 1944. He saw his best friend die before he reached the shore. There were fifty-nine men in B Troop: fifty marines, six sergeants, and three officers. By the end of that long day the troop had fought their way off the beach and into town. There were only seventeen men left, and at eighteen years old Anthony Rubinstein, the equivalent of a private, was in command.

3.

Alaska, the Fourth Day

I WENT TO ALASKA KNOWING IT WOULDN'T BE EASY. I DIDN'T WANT it to be. I went alone, hoping to test myself and to find adventure among strangers. The brochure for the month-long wilderness survival course had offered several locations, but only for Alaska did it state, in a bold stamp across the page, "**Be Prepared for a Maximum in Physical and Emotional Stress.**" At the time, I was fascinated by physical courage, and I was anxious to know if I would have it when it mattered. "Maximum" was an attractive word.

We gathered in Whittier, a one-building town on Prince William Sound. I was the youngest; I would turn seventeen two weeks later, without fanfare, on a cold day in August. We spent a month training, every day paddling further into the wilderness. Our time was filled with lessons. We learned to build fires in the rain. We learned to cook in coals. We learned to bake underground. Because doing anything else seemed a waste of time, we learned to eat the swarming mosquitoes that landed on our food (they don't taste bad, sort of sweet). We learned to navigate by

9

map and compass, we learned mountaineering and seamanship, we learned group decision-making, and we learned about the local flora and fauna. We learned, all day, every day.

And then the training ended, and the real lessons began. The instructors chose leaders from among the students, based mostly on who would gain the most from the leadership experience. At the mouth of a glaciated bay full of icebergs and seals, eighty miles from Whittier, we were broken into small groups and assigned our leaders. The groups then plotted their way home, charting their course through the scattered islands of Prince William Sound. I was put in a group with Rick, Bonnie, and Cathy. Rick would be my tent mate, and Bonnie would be our leader. Bonnie was a slight woman in her early thirties, reserved and quiet. Not an obvious choice, but when her leadership moment came, she would rise to meet it. Rick was in college, a big burly guy from New York. Cathy was a year older than me, a girl next door from Ohio.

Hours after the groups were assigned, a fishing trawler pulled up offshore. Our instructors took all our food, boarded the boat, and waved goodbye. See you back in Whittier in four days.

The first three days were hard. In the endless drizzle we paddled twelve hours a day. We were clad in wool—even our underwear was wool. We slept in wool. The wool was always wet, and the sky was always gray. On day one and day two we could only find mussels to eat. My body does not tolerate mussels, so I went without. While paddling Rick and I repeatedly sang ditties from fast food restaurants to dream away our hunger: "Two all-beef patties special sauce lettuce cheese pickles onions on a sesame seed bun." Cathy and Bonnie did not seem impressed with our performance; perhaps they were not musically inclined. On the third day, in a gathering storm, no one ate; it didn't seem worth the effort required, and the sky was getting increasingly ominous. We were all anxious about what the next day would bring; we had a two-mile open water passage before us, and it was not clear that we should attempt it.

In the middle of the night, in the first hours of the fourth day, the storm arrived. When I remember that fourth day now, I am always there, in the present.

It has been raining for ten days, but the howling wind is new. The tent twists and flaps in the gale, then collapses on top of us. Rick and I lie on the stone beach in the pitch black; wet, cold, and too tired to move. We stay in our sleeping bags. We don't talk until later, when we hear the rushing water and then feel it start to flow around us. We are camped in a previously dry stream bed that runs to the sea, a rookie mistake. Rick struggles to get out of his bag. There is something wrong with him, and it is getting worse. We can barely make out the shape of the other tent through the sheets of rain; it still stands. We do not pitch our tent again; we just move it and climb into the collapsed tangle of fabric. There will be no more sleep. The weather keeps getting worse; every piece of gear and clothing we have is soaked. Things are not going well.

And then dawn arrives. The wind has slackened a little, and the rain is back to its drizzle. But the sea is rough, and Rick's health continues to deteriorate. Now he has white stuff on the skin around his mouth, and he is getting weaker. I am running out of energy; my hunger is replaced by a dull tiredness. Walking up a small rise to bury the latrine, I lose my balance and fall, a strange side effect of the calorie shortage. We pack the gear in the boats grimly, at this point just shoving stuff in, and we set off down the coast. At the tip of the island, we pull the boats together and confer. The open passage has heavy chop, but the wind will be behind us. We decide that we don't really have another option, so we paddle out. It quickly becomes clear that a current is taking us south, and south is where we don't want to go. With some urgency we decide to strap the boats together and use the paddles and a tent fly to make a sail. Much to our delight, this unrehearsed trick works. We are back on course, running before the wind, and we cheer as the next island grows quickly before us. A loud crack wipes the smile from our faces. A paddle has snapped, and the tent fly has torn free on one side. We immediately grasp the seriousness of our situation, and in fearful haste, we get out our extra paddle and dig for shore. The current is still strong, and we are slowly moving down the side of the island to a place where the waves batter against the cliffs. We paddle as hard as we can. As the cliffs approach, with a last push, we run the boats up at the end of the rocky beach.

We are tired and Rick needs help to stand, so we make a mistake and leave the boats at the water's edge while we set out to find a camp spot. The wind eases and the sun breaks through the clouds; our spirits lift with its warmth. Before us the dense evergreen forest runs down to a strip of waist-high sea grass, which in turn gives way to the smooth black stones of the beach. The cliffs rise to our south and there is a forested headland to our north. The water is white, tinged in blue, glacial milk from the ice field beyond the cliffs. Further out, the darker Pacific stretches to the snow-clad peaks of the horizon. I marvel at the splendor; there is no sign that man lives on earth.

As we turn back to the boats, it becomes obvious that we are not alone. An odd-looking animal is loping down the beach toward us. He is powerfully built; he looks like a cross between a German Shepherd and a small bear, with big jaws and an undersized square head. He makes his teeth visible. As he comes toward us, I slowly reach down and pick up a large rock. About thirty feet away he stops. He rears up, his front legs on a driftwood log, and snarls. You can feel the saliva more than you see it; his incisors are long and sharp; he is fearsome. Now we stare at each other, him with his teeth and me with my rock. Seconds tick by, then he turns and jogs off, back the way he came.

We cannot stay on our hard-won beach. We are now among the lucky humans who have seen a wolverine in the wild, but we agree that he might be a she, and she might have cubs. In any case, there is no question that we have been warned off.

As we load back into the kayaks, we note that some water has splashed in during our landing, or during our foray up the beach. No matter, it is time to go. That, after all, was a wolverine. We push back out into the surf and paddle straight out. We make it over the first big roller, but the second one takes us a bit sideways, and the sluggish boat rolls over. Glacial milk is extremely cold. I come back to the surface breathless, my chest constricted. I help Bonnie lie across the boat; she seems stunned. It is only forty yards to shore but I have on layers of wool, waterproof gear, and high rubber boots. Swimming the boat to shore seems to take forever— my legs aren't working right. Rick turns the other boat and paddles for shore; Cathy is screaming, high pitched and desperate.

We make it back to the beach. Rick is lying on the rocks over-come by whatever it is that ails him. Cathy is huddled, her arms wrapped around her knees, head down, crying. I sit on a piece of driftwood, empty in every sense of the word. Bonnie comes to me and reports the other two are nonfunctional. She claims I need to help her unpack the boats, empty them of water, and pack them up again. I don't respond. She tells me again. I am in some other place; I no longer care. Bonnie smacks me across the face. Hard. It is a slap, but she gives it all she has. I nod, get up, and the two of us unload and reload the boats. The job done, we stand facing the sea, ready to push off. It is difficult to force myself back into the water, but there is no choice. The four of us paddle back through the surf, around the headland, and find another beach. There is no wolverine, and the storm has blown itself out.

The next day we load the boats for the final push. We practically carry Rick down to the water and set out for Whittier. The water is calm; we paddle in weak silence. When we land, the instructors take one look at Rick and rush him to the clinic. The rest of us join the breakfast on the beach for the small groups as they arrive. Nobody wants the food; we all just want a hot shower. While I wait my turn, I try to eat a donut. I can't swallow and only manage to choke down a small piece. Good news comes back from the clinic: Rick is on an IV, suffering from advanced dehydration. He had been so wet, for so long, that he forgot to drink.

Finally, it is my turn for the bathroom, and I get to see my face for the first time in a month. I look different. I have my first beard; it is a scraggly thing. My cheeks are hollow, and my hair is matted. The baby fat is gone for now; I have lost twenty-five pounds. I step into the hot shower. No shower will ever feel that good again.

PART II
Early Years

Sales rep to CEO: seventeen years, five companies, eleven jobs, sixteen bosses. D. Van Nostrand, meeting Connie, Doubleday, Checkerboard Press, Simon & Schuster, a career change that didn't happen, my daughter, being an author, Dorling Kindersley, my son.

1979–1996

I.

On the Road

M Y FIRST JOB AFTER COLLEGE WAS IN SEATTLE, WORKING for a small publisher named D. Van Nostrand. I was a college traveler, a salesman selling textbooks to professors. The traveler title was apt; I had a vast territory stretching from the northwest corner of Washington to the southeast corner of Colorado. I travelled only by car, an old-style station wagon. Twice a year I would fill it with book samples and sporting equipment and head east. A single loop of the territory took a little more than three months, and ever conscious of expenses, I stayed in the cheapest motels I could find. A Motel 6 was a night of luxury.

It was 1979. The best available technology for my job was a box briefcase, a calculator, and a landline phone; the fax, answering machine, and cell phone were still years away. Every week I was on the road I could cash a travel letter at a local bank for up to $300 to cover my expenses. Staying in touch with the office meant a lot of time on payphones, reverse the charges please.

I worked hard, and I got business from far-flung community colleges that previous travelers had never visited. It was not great for my social life—"Nice to meet you, I'll be back in three months"—but it was good for my skiing. I was bored by the massive volume of paperwork, so I took to sending in my call reports on humorous, mostly tacky postcards. I figured they would enjoy them in the office, and it allowed me to make the reports very short. I generally misbehaved at sales conference and otherwise gently broke the rules. But by the end of my first year, sales in my territory were up, I was deemed a success, and they promoted me to field manager.

In early March 1981, I loaded up my car for my fourth major loop through the territory. The professors were more familiar now, there was lots of snow in the mountains, and if things went well, I had a decent shot at a nice bonus for my trouble. I was hoping for a good trip. I started at Mission Ridge Community College and worked my way eastward: Spokane, Cheney, Coeur d'Alene, Missoula, Bozeman. On a fine spring Friday, I arrived on the campus of Eastern Montana State University in Billings. After lunch in the student cafeteria, I went outside and found a payphone. It was next to the door, on a brick wall in the sun. I called the office to report in, and the assistant in the sales department promptly asked, "Where in the hell have you been?" I cheerfully responded that I had been out selling and . . . She cut me off mid-sentence and said, "Steve needs to talk to you." Steve Kraham was my boss, the VP of sales. He was an old school sales guy, who constantly had one of those fake plastic cigarettes in his hand. For two years he had been using it to help him quit smoking, and there was no end in sight. He had blue eyes that twinkled when he was waving that cigarette around, and he was in constant good humor.

Steve came on the line quickly and asked, "Where in the hell have you been?" Again, I tried to explain the rigors of my travel, and again I was cut short. Steve said, "Look, I have bad news and I have worse news. The bad news is that the company has been sold to Thompson, and they have eliminated our entire sales force to save money. Your job no longer exists."

Stunned, I asked, "If that is the bad news, what could be worse?"

He replied, "Actually, you were fired two weeks ago."

I hung up, got in the car, and headed home to the ranch. A week later I made my way back to Seattle, and that fall I moved back east to chase an MBA. I didn't make my bonus.

2.

Who's Pete?

I N MY FIRST YEAR OF GRADUATE SCHOOL IN NEW YORK CITY, I HAD two great pursuits: playing sports and finding a girlfriend. Unfortunately, I was ill suited for both, and I had a track record to prove it.

Over the years I had been on many basketball and rugby teams, usually playing third string or riding the pine. In addition, I had worn out a lot of shoes running slowly. In high school, I ran cross-country for three years and never missed a race. In all that time, I had a single moment of glory. It happened during the last race of my senior year. I was halfway up the daunting hill at the end of our course, my legs burning, my breathing ragged. But then I saw a runner in front of me, and he was struggling. It might be possible. I slowly gained ground, and when we topped the hill, I was twenty yards back. He didn't know I was there. With fifty yards left I emptied my tank in a final sprint. He heard me coming, but too late. With a couple yards to go, I passed him. For three years I finished last in every single race. On this final day I was second to last. A victory of sorts.

With girls, I was even slower. I managed to make it through high school without a date, and with a few short-lived exceptions, that trend continued. I fell heavily for girls, and they always seemed to like me right back . . . as a friend. I was that nice guy who finished last.

But these things can change. On a fine New York day in the early summer of 1982, I got out of class early and decided to walk the six blocks to my favorite lunch spot, Koronet Pizza. I ate my slices on the bench in the middle of Broadway, enjoying the sun. Well satisfied, I went down the stairs at the 110th Street subway station and hopped on the downtown Broadway local.

The subway car was mostly full. Looking left, I spied an empty seat next to a short-haired girl in a sleeveless green shirt. She was effortlessly beautiful. She was also significantly above my pay grade. I sat next to her silently, eyes ahead. She didn't look up; she was intent on reading a letter. Glancing over, I noticed it was signed, "Please come back. I love you. Pete." She put the letter away and I screwed up my courage. "So . . . who's Pete?" She seemed startled. She didn't smile, but she was friendly. We chatted briefly and discovered that we were both at the same school. My stop came. I had never asked a girl for her number before, and I realized there was no chance I could do it now. I got up and with an awkward little wave walked out of the subway car, kicking myself.

Connie would report much later that she knew I was the guy for her when I walked onto the train. Something about the shoes. For the record, New Balance, back when New Balance was new. Thankfully she had more skills than I did in matters of the heart. She would wait by the mailboxes at school and act surprised when we saw each other, but not overly interested. During the next few weeks, one way or the other, she managed to get the ball rolling. On July 4 weekend we had a date. A miracle on 110th Street.

In October, I broke some ribs on the rugby field, effectively ending my career in team sports. I ran the New York City Marathon in November but would never run another. Connie, on the other hand, was going to stick around for the long term.

In the first week of January, I went to work at Doubleday, the family firm. I went with a cautious sort of optimism, a hope for what it might be, and a vague sense of what might go wrong. I had a tough commute and a low salary, but there was lots of joy. I had a girlfriend.

3.

If Beale Street Could Talk

R OYALTY DEPARTMENTS INVARIABLY FALL SHORT OF THEIR
name; there is nothing much royal about them. They are usually found in the back corner of publishing houses, far from the
glamour of the editors. They are the complex underbelly of publishing, where debits and credits determine the size of the checks the
authors receive. At Doubleday the royalty department was a vast
square of gray desks housed in an old printing plant in Garden City,
Long Island. It was a few yards down the hall from where I worked.

I was an eager young financial analyst doing the daily three-
train schlep out from New York City. Shortly after I started in the
job, someone in the New York office claimed there was a problem
with James Baldwin's royalties. I was assigned the task of recon-
ciling decades of his royalty statements. The files arrived at my
desk in short order—boxes filled with Xeroxed accounting records
known as royalty cards, along with the statements we had sent to
the author. I gamely plowed into the stack, starting with the book
If Beale Street Could Talk.

This was in 1983. The ancient phones in the Garden City office were still rotary, and every desk had an adding machine. Yes, a mechanical adding machine, the electric ones with the little roll of paper. I entered the numbers from the first column of the *Beale Street* royalty card, hunt-and-peck style, and pulled the bar on the side to total. The total did not match what was on the royalty card. It wasn't even close. And none of the other columns added up either. Completely mystified, I took a stack of the Xeroxes and went in search of the legendary Jerry Weatherall.

Jerry was a good accountant, a manager who had been in the royalty department for twenty-five years. He was gracious and unflappable, and he remembered everything. I explained my problem. Jerry gave me a knowing smile and said we would have to look at the original royalty cards, not the Xeroxes. Off we went to the back room, where Jerry pointed to some file drawers and left me to it. I quickly discovered why they were called royalty cards. They were handwritten on card stock, not paper. From the original cards, the problem became obvious. The columns on each card contained numbers in black for royalties earned by the author, and numbers in red for payments made to the author. Xeroxes in those days were still black and white, so there was no way to know I should have been subtracting the red numbers.

In a normal case, this problem would have been discernible: one large number for the author advance (red) and smaller numbers for the royalties the author earned (black). But for Baldwin there were dozens of red numbers, mostly for small amounts. How could he keep getting advances? Back to Jerry Weatherall. I got another Jerry smile: "You might try the backup files." There I found an entire filing drawer that explained the red numbers, the unusual payments to James Baldwin. It seems that Baldwin led a complex life, and that his expenses often outpaced his royalty earnings. The file contained his requests for money, and the signed approvals to pay. Fifty dollars here, a hundred dollars there. Basically, when

Baldwin ran out of cash, he would make a request to his publisher so he could pay off his debts. In his requests, there was a window into his large life, and in the approvals you could see the goodwill and good sense of his publisher.

Jerry was resistant to spill the beans behind the requests, but I finally got him to share some details. It led me to read *If Beale Street Could Talk* and to enjoy Baldwin's extraordinary talent. It also made me realize accountants generally know more than they say. When I finally got the red numbers and black numbers right, I discovered all the columns on all the cards totaled correctly. There had never been a problem.

Four years later, though there would be a problem, it would be my problem, and it would have nothing to do with Mr. Baldwin.

4.

ALF and Other Strange Creatures

I NEEDED A NEW JOB. I WAS TWENTY-EIGHT YEARS OLD, AND THE doors were closing for me at Doubleday. I thought I would spend my career at the company, but the guy who ran the place, my uncle, clearly had a different view. I had refused to approve an invoice for payment, he was irritated, and perhaps the family baggage was just getting too heavy. Realizing that I had better move on, I polished up my resume. An editor friend, Lisa Drew, got me an interview with Larry Hughes at William Morrow. Larry gave me sage advice, but he didn't have a job for me. With kind words and generosity, he sent me on to see Norman Pomerance at Harper and Jeremiah Kaplan, the president of Macmillan Publishing (a completely different company from the Macmillan of today).

I arrived for my interview with Jerry Kaplan at Macmillan's Third Avenue offices. I stood nervously at his open door. Without looking up or saying a word, he waved me to a chair in front of his desk. He continued to read some papers as we sat together in the long silence. Stealing a glance, I realized he was reading a letter from Larry Hughes and then my resume, and he was focused on every word. Finally, he looked up at me with unwavering eyes. There were no pleasantries. "So why does Larry Hughes think you are any good?" A tough start by any measure. After I fumbled the answer, he asked his next question: "Moving from sales to the business side is just stupid. Why did you do that?" I started to sweat.

It went on like that for a half an hour. Then he grabbed his phone, called a guy named Steve, and asked him to join us. Steve turned out to be Steve Addams, Macmillan's CFO. Jerry pointed to me and said, "This is John Sargent; I'm going to give him the new thing."

Steve lifted an eyebrow, "Really?"

Jerry assured him it was going to be fine and told me I would start two weeks from Monday, reporting to Steve. Alarmed at the pace of the conversation, I asked, "But wait, what is the new thing?" Jerry explained it was a company they had just bought, and that he couldn't tell me the name yet. I would be working on the acquisition, and then in operations afterward. I said that I needed to know more, small things like what the company did, what the job would be, what I would be paid, and what title I would have.

He gave me a short answer: "It's a good job, and you will make more than you do now. Just say yes."

Two weeks later I arrived at work and was shown to Steve's office. He looked up, clearly puzzled. Then recognition dawned and he asked, "Damn, are you starting today?" I answered in the affirmative. He stood and came to the door, looked around, and then cleared some space on the corner of his assistant's desk. He pulled up a visitor's chair and handed me a pile of reports. "Here you go, read these." I shared that desk for my first week, a two-foot by two-foot piece of desktop with no drawers. The next week I got my own little desk. It was pushed together with another one just like it, and two of us shared a phone. The guy sitting next to us was actually in a closet.

The new thing turned out to be Rand McNally children's books. After the acquisition, we named the company Checkerboard Press, and we set it up as a stand-alone entity within Macmillan Inc. My job was "everything that isn't sales, marketing, and editorial." An odd job description, and a job for which I had scant qualification.

I worked long hours and I generally did well, though I made a series of mistakes early on. I set up a warehouse and an invoicing system. I scoured every invoice, but then forgot to focus on collecting the money customers owed us. I ignored the art director's proofs and changed the color of some book covers on press. I thought they looked better my way. I took the Newbery Medal sticker off the jacket of *Misty of Chincoteague* to save a few bucks. The author was devastaded. I added an arbitrary cushion to the cost of every book we printed, just in case we needed it. Never mind those pesky debits and credits.

Despite my occasional bumbling, we were instantly successful, based almost entirely on my new boss, Terry Savoy, and his completely intuitive early commitment to . . . ALF. Yes, we sold millions of coloring books based on a TV alien with a phallic nose, our proud contribution to the literature of the 1980s.[1] Success brought a host of problems, and our tiny staff struggled mightily to get the work done and to comply with Macmillan's corporate demands. And so, even with our alien-charged good results, we had some trepidation when we arrived at our first corporate business review.

It was my first board meeting of any kind. Ned Evans, the chairman and controlling shareholder, was there. He wore sunglasses the whole time and was constantly touching the sides of his nose. His body would occasionally shake a bit, and he would regularly

---

1   ALF was a very successful family sitcom which ran from 1986 to 1990. There was also an animated prequel. ALF stood for Alien Life Form.

snuffle; it was not clear that he had slept the night before. Jerry Kaplan was there. He had a vast and quirky intelligence, a kindly enthusiasm, and loose skin like a bulldog. When distracted, he would roll big wrinkles of that skin up the side of his face. On this day he was distracted a lot. Lester Rakoff, the corporate controller, was there. He was a good man and a great accountant. He also had a medical condition that caused him to twitch and, when under stress, to twitch aggressively.

At times these odd shakings, twitchings, and rollings would happen serially, at times all together. I watched in wonder. I knew publishing was full of characters, but I had never considered oddities at this scale, all gathered together in a corporate boardroom. ALF would have fit in well.

I attended only one more board meeting at Checkerboard Press, and it was a relatively normal affair. Then Jerry Kaplan moved on to a job at Simon & Schuster, and after a few months I was asked to join him.

A couple of decades later, comfortably ensconced at a different Macmillan, I forced myself to watch a video of a speech I had just delivered. I was immediately alarmed. Where did that twang come from? Why was I scratching my head? Then halfway through the video, seemingly with a purpose, I inserted my left index finger into my ear. Apparently, I do that with regularity. It wasn't a shake, a twitch, or a roll, but it certainly was strange. I learned from the best.

5.

Dick and the Duchess

I WAS IN THE CONTRACTS DEPARTMENT IN THE SIMON & SCHUSTER building, working on a deal and talking with a young manager. The phone rang on her desk. She picked it up, listened, and the color slowly drained from her face. She handed me the phone across the desk. "It's Dick Snyder, and he is looking for you."

I took the phone to hear Dick's gravel voice issue a short command: "Sargent, get up here now. You are going to start earning your money."

When I decided to take the job running the Children's Book Division at Dick Snyder's S&S, Terry Savoy gave me two pieces of advice. First, he said not to worry when I got fired, because everyone at S&S gets fired. Second, he warned me that Dick was a bully: "If Snyder starts to yell at you, move in close, look down at him, and ball up your fist." A practical approach, but I struggled to visualize it in the office.

The job I signed up for was going to be difficult. Children's Books was a small division in a very large company, it lost money every year, and eight different people had failed to run it success-fully in the last seven years. None of those people were still with the company. Dick had decided to give up and sell the division, but he had just hired Jerry Kaplan to be the president of S&S, and Jerry convinced him to give it one more try: "There is this kid . . . "

At previous jobs I had always had a desk, a cubicle, or a small standard office. When I arrived at S&S, they assigned me a huge corner office with built-in bookshelves and cabinets, hardwood flooring, and two walls of gracious windows overlooking the ice rink in Rockefeller Center. It came with a key to my own bath-room, which I promptly gave to our pregnant receptionist. I sat five floors directly below Dick Snyder himself. It was 1987, and at twenty-nine years of age, I was a newly minted publisher.

A few months into the job I was invited to an employee cock-tail party. A nice guy I had met a few weeks before named Michael Selleck pulled me aside and explained that if I wanted to succeed here, I needed Italian suits (later he explained that I needed shoes that had laces as well). I looked over the room full of people, who were indeed extremely well dressed, and saw Dick Snyder, the great man himself. He was in a tailored suit with suspenders, and he was waving me over. He introduced himself, looked me up and down, and growled, "I fired the guy before you, I fired the guy before him, and I fired the guy before that. I hope I don't have to fire you." In answer to my stunned silence, he said, "I tell you what. One year from now we're gonna have a party. Either we will celebrate your success, or we will be saying goodbye."

That was the last exchange I had with him before the contracts department call. In a hurry, I rode the elevator to the seventeenth floor. The reception area was large and formal; the company logo, the Sower, was the pattern in the carpet. Dick's office suite included a dining room, a bathroom, a gym, and a palatial office. I was escorted to his door, and Dick, staying seated, gestured to the chair facing his desk. He promptly leaned back, put his feet on that desk, crossed them, and showed me the leather soles of his fancy shoes. He bellowed, "Nancy!" His assistant came in carrying a silver tray. On the silver tray rested a single cigarette. He took the lonely smoke, Nancy lit it, and after a long drag, Dick explained, "I'm trying to quit so I have her bring them in one at a time."

Dick told me I was doing a great job, but now we were going to see what I was made of. He told me he had made a secret deal with Sarah Ferguson, the Duchess of York, who had decided to write children's books. Her agent was the legendary Mort Janklow, Dick's favorite power player in publishing. My job would be to negotiate the details of the deal and to work with our UK operation to publish the book globally. No one, and he was very clear on this, no one, could know about the project until the Duchess decided we could announce it. He told me that I needed to find a way to hide the amount we were paying her from everyone, and forever. He told me the amount, and I tried not to show the shock I felt.

I was worried when I left Dick's office. First, successfully negotiating a major deal with Janklow was probably a bit beyond me. Then there was the matter of the money. Further, at the time, children's books were not written by celebrities, and the Duchess's celebrity was already tainted. There was little precedent for how to do this.

The deal itself was simple enough. The Duchess had just gotten her helicopter license and loved to fly. She would write two picture books featuring a helicopter character named Budgie. We would find her a few illustrators, and she would choose one to work on the book. There was a publicity clause in the contract; she would have to promote the books. We would get a percentage of merchandise rights. And most importantly, the Duchess committed to giving a portion of all the proceeds to charity.

I worked with our UK office, and they assigned Denise Johnstone Bert to be the editor. I didn't have to manage the process of getting the books written and illustrated; a good thing, as the Duchess wanted to be fully involved in the details. My job was to handle all the other issues globally, starting with creating the financial system to ensure the advance could never be traced. Denise was trained by the palace on proper royal etiquette, and she trained me.

Denise and the Duchess chose an illustrator, and the Duchess flew him around in a helicopter to give him perspective and context for drawing Budgie. By all reports, it was not your standard author/illustrator experience.

The time came for me to write directly to our new author. I was required to use the salutation "Your Royal Highness." That seemed reasonable enough. But I was also required to sign off, "I remain your most humble and obedient servant." No chance I was going to do that. There ensued a flurry of communication with the United Kingdom. Perhaps I didn't understand. I most certainly didn't. I avoided writing until the day I had to, and I can still recall my queasiness when I finally wrote those words.

We knew that the books would require extraordinary publicity, ideally the highest-rated interview show on television. At the time that was a Barbara Walters special. To make it work, we would need a commitment for the special up front, but we couldn't share what the books were, nor the identity of the author. Feeling a bit unsettled about the whole thing, I tracked down the name of a producer for Barbara Walters at ABC. I called the producer and explained that I controlled an interview with a member of the royal family. I informed her I could not tell her why I controlled the interview, or which member of the royal family it was. She said ABC would not be interested. Feeling a bit desperate I said, "She is a major royal." That got me nowhere. I asked to speak to Barbara and was informed that would not be possible, and furthermore, Barbara was out of town on vacation. I hung up with a feeling of dread. Fifteen minutes later, the phone rang. I picked up with my usual "John Sargent" and heard that unmistakable voice,

"Hi John, this is Barbara Walters." I gave her a series of hints, she committed to a prime time special on the spot, and she let me choose the date.

The two books were close to finished, and though we worried a bit about the art, we had high hopes. We chose a publication date based on the Duchess's travel schedule and her commitments in the United Kingdom. We agreed on a date to announce the publication, and to show the world the book jackets. Then, after some back and forth with the Buckingham Palace press staff, we launched *Budgie the Little Helicopter* into the world.

In the preceding months the press coverage of the Duchess had turned from bad to vicious. They had recently dubbed her Big Fat Fergie; the gloves were off. But we felt Budgie would be a positive story—how could a princess writing books for children be anything else? We hoped it would get a warm reception, particularly as we would also announce the Duchess of York would be giving a portion of the proceeds to charity. There was no such luck. Unknown to us, the royal family is paid to be royal by the state, and no one is allowed to make money on commercial ventures. The intense focus of the Budgie story became the size of the charitable contribution. The palace was deluged with press calls. They decided not to comment and told the press if they had any questions they should talk to John Sargent at Simon & Schuster. To be helpful, they provided my phone number.

We were a small division of Simon & Schuster. Forty people or so, dedicated to publishing books for young children, mostly sold through bookstores and libraries. Our publicity department was set up to get book reviews and to promote authors. To get to profitability, we had been through a round of layoffs and had instituted very tight cost controls. There were no resources to deal with what Budgie would bring us.

After the announcement, my phone rang constantly. The British tabloid reporters were fantastically creative and relentless, posing as all sorts of people to try and get information. The US reporters also stretched the limits of reasonable ethics. A major TV network wanted to interview the Duchess on her trip to South Africa, and of course my wife and I would need to be there, and the network would pick up the entire tab for a weeklong first-class trip. Wow, but no thank you.

In the United Kingdom, the story just kept growing, and it was entirely negative. Then, out of nowhere, a claim surfaced that the Duchess had copied the idea for Budgie from a book called *Hector the Helicopter*. With that, the press office at Buckingham Palace had seen enough. They called and said the Duchess would not be coming to the United States to promote her book. I responded that they couldn't do that, and I would fly over immediately to discuss it. The time was set for two days hence, in the morning. I was about to go on my first international business trip, for a meeting in Buckingham Palace no less, but there was nothing in the budget to pay for it.

I asked my assistant to find the very cheapest flight and a hotel room for a single night at under a hundred bucks, as close to the palace as possible. Remarkably, she found a cheap flight and a hotel room, reasonably close to the palace, for seventy pounds.

I called the palace to confirm the date and time. They asked for my hotel in case the Duchess had a last-minute change in plans. I provided the name and address. They informed me that there must be some mistake. I said, "I don't think so, I am reading it from the confirmation."

There was a pause, then an icy "Very well, then."

I flew over the next day and arrived late at night. The hotel was a complete dive. The room was just big enough for the single bed, and the bathroom was a sink in the corner. After a few hours of sleep, I was up early and off to the palace. As it turns out, when you have a meeting at Buckingham Palace, you enter in the front, by the fountain. Who knew? The cab dropped me at the famous gates, my name was on a list, and I was sent to the front door. The Duchess's equerry met me at reception. As we walked up the grand staircase to the second floor, he asked me how my trip had been. I responded that it had been fine. He paused on a step, turned toward me, and with a slight smirk asked, "How was your hotel?" I was halfway through telling him about the place when he started laughing. "You do know that is a hotel for prostitutes?"

From the top of the stairs, we walked the length of the building. It was a vast hallway, portraits hanging on the wall to the right, magnificent windows overlooking the fountain on the left. He stopped in front of an unmarked door and knocked. I heard a muffled voice say to come in. He swung the door open, and we stepped into the Duke and Duchess's apartment. Spacious. Comfortable. A nice view. A corner apartment in Buckingham Palace.

She rushed toward me, beaming. She grabbed my hand in both of hers. "John, it is so very good to finally see you!" She was a couple of years younger than me, casually dressed, no discernible make up. I had been trained to say, "I'm pleased to meet you, Your Royal Highness." Instead, I responded, "Hey, it's great to see you, too!"[2]

The equerry left us and we sat in her apartment for a while. There were pictures of Andrew about, and she referred to him as "My Prince." He was off in the Navy, and she clearly missed him. She was incredibly open, enthusiastic, and bawdy. Finally getting to business, I asked if she wanted to come to New York to promote her book. She replied, "Of course I do, but they won't let me." It was clear to me she was not fond of "they."

The time came for the scheduled meeting, and we filed into the conference room next door. It was nice, but clearly meant for

---

2   This was a constant issue. She always called herself Sarah, as in, "Hi John, it's Sarah." I settled on using no name when at all possible and Ma'am when I had to use something. Toward the end, I just gave up and called her Sarah.

business. The Duchess sat at the head of the table, her equerry and me on one side, a host of palace staff on the other. I noted that they called her Your Royal Highness, and it was sincere. The head of the palace contingent was Robin Janvrin, the press secretary to the Queen. He was a generation older and distinguished. He emanated power and intelligence. A man of the world.

I told Robin that the Duchess had to come to New York; plans had been made and canceling would be viewed badly by the press. He explained that the story had to die. Now. The Duchess would be staying in London. The conversation quickly got heated. Finally, I said that I had a great respect for their opinions and expertise, but I had a contract that was signed by the Duchess, and it required her to be in New York. "I don't intend to offer any relief from that contract."

There was a notable silence.

The conversation started again, and we began to discuss how things might work. We talked about what we should say, and what we shouldn't. Finally, we all agreed that a short trip to New York would be manageable. The palace staff filtered out; Robin was the last to go. I noted that he backed out of the room, bowed to the Duchess, and said, "Good day, Your Royal Highness." I wondered how painful that was for him, and how much it must have warped her over time.

The Duchess and I said our goodbyes. As I walked out, I was surprised to see Robin waiting down the hall. He asked if he could have a word. He apologized for being difficult; he understood it was about business for me. He explained that the royal family was different from anything I had ever experienced: "Think of it this way, John. The royal family is like a Fortune 500 company, but in this case all of the management are relatives, and many of them are in-laws." And then he told me that the Duchess of York was the single greatest threat to the monarchy in the current era, and his job was to control that threat. He feared her lack of grace and popularity would stain them all. If I had been on my game, I would have replied, "God save the Queen."

I walked down the hall further and stopped for a brief chat with the equerry, a nice guy with a difficult job. He took me down a back stairway, and then pointed me to the front door. I moved quickly; I was starting to run late for the flight home. As I reached the door, a security guy stuck his arm out and told me to wait. I was a bit annoyed and asked him why. He looked at me and nodded at the door. I looked out and there was the Buckingham Palace changing of the guard. I stood and stared at the splendor for a moment, but then thought of my flight. "How long will this take?" He replied that it shouldn't be more than a few minutes. That seemed odd. The plaza in front of the palace was entirely full of the Queen's Guards, marching in their bearskin helmets. Then the formations suddenly came to a halt, the Guards stood at rigid attention, and the officers started barking commands. The security guy tapped me on the shoulder and said, "You can go now, sir." I gave him a puzzled look and he said, "Don't worry, they will be at attention for a few minutes, walk straight through them and out the gate." OK. It was late summer and the front of the palace and the fountain beyond were swarmed with tourists who were watching the proceedings and taking pictures. As calmly as I could, I walked between two long rows of men, their uniforms immaculate. They were rigid and silent, their eyes locked forward. I was awestruck and trying hard not to show it. As I got to the gate, I could hear hundreds of cameras snapping, many pointed at me. There was a bobby at the gate; he swung it open a bit so I could get out.

He gave me a grin and said, "That was pretty good, eh?" Yes, it was.

Back in New York preparations for the publication began in earnest. The Duchess would be in town for three days and two nights. Our goal was to gain the support of the children's book community who were skeptical of the books and to inform the public of Budgie's imminent arrival. The number one priority was not to go broke paying for it all.

I took on the task of finding the Duchess a hotel room. Hotels in New York do not have royal suites, but her office was anxious that she have the best accommodations at the best hotel. I suspected they were a bit worried because of my hotel choice in London. I went to five of the best hotels in New York, met with the general managers, and got tours of their presidential suites. During a long call with the palace, we decided on the Hotel Plaza Athénée as a discreet and less showy option. I met with the general manager for a second time and explained that he would get lots of press both before and during her stay, and that therefore she should get the presidential suite for free. He was not buying what I was selling, but we settled on a number I could live with.

Now that we could use her name, we arranged a live interview with the *Today Show*, and they agreed to come to her hotel. We set up a cocktail party in the Rainbow Room for that evening. We committed her to host the opening of the Children's Museum on the Upper West Side of Manhattan. In between the book events the palace organized a visit to a school in a tough neighborhood and other royal duties. It was a packed schedule.

The books were printed at this point, locked down under tight security. The British tabloid press was in a frenzy. There was one reporter who camped out in a bar across the street from the printer, offering cash to anyone who would smuggle out a copy.

The Secret Service arrived for what they called a reccy (short for reconnaissance, I was told). This involved a tour of every place the Duchess would be going in order to determine escape routes and get the lay of the land. There was an inordinate fascination about the availability of bathrooms. Since the Duchess was scheduled to meet Dick Snyder, this allowed me a tour of his private bathroom, a place often discussed but generally never seen by those who worked for him.

Eventually I discovered the reason for the bathroom obsession: the Duchess was pregnant. Connie was also pregnant at the time. Unfortunately, Connie's pregnancy was not going well, and she was on enforced bedrest. This required me to prepare six small meals every day before leaving for work. It also allowed her to watch the unfolding Budgie saga on TV.

At last, publication day arrived and so did the Duchess. She had remarkable stamina and energy. I was her escort, while others were deployed to the various venues. The Barbara Walters special aired, and it was great. The trip to the Children's Museum was in a motorcade up Sixth Avenue. The Duchess laughed at my school-boy grin when they hit the lights and sirens. She was mischievous and teasing, but you could also see the stress she was under. At one point she told me about her money woes, now common knowledge but at that time unthinkable for a member of the royal family. She asked if we could pay her more upfront; I was mortified and said we couldn't.

The next day we had the *Today Show* interview in the hotel with Jane Pauley. The production folks were set up early. Lights, cameras, hair, and makeup. It was show time. The room was hot from the lights and getting hotter. But there was no Duchess. Jane looked at me and said, "We are ready to go here, where is she?" With a knot in my gut, I went in search of Her Royal Highness. I discovered she had left the hotel early that morning to go see an art exhibit downtown. I found the State Department security guy waiting on the sidewalk in front of the hotel. We stood there together. I knew that he was not allowed to discuss where she was.

I kept asking him, "When will she return? Is she on her way?" Finally, after watching me pace anxiously, he told me she was in the hotel and had been for a while.

I ran to her suite, and it is no exaggeration to say I pounded on her door. One of her staff answered and I demanded, "Where in the hell is she?" There was a brief pause and then a confession that she was having trouble deciding which shoes to wear. I managed to make clear that we needed to go. Right now. The Duchess complied. I could see that the *Today Show* staff was ticked off when we came in, but Jane was professional. The Duchess was calm and did well. I was wrung out.

We went to the S&S offices that afternoon. She signed some books and then we went upstairs to see Dick. We came off the elevator and there he was, much to my surprise, standing at reception to meet her. Mr. Tough Guy was gone. This was a new Dick. After weeks of telling me, "I'm not doing any of that Your Royal Highness crap," he greeted her with "Welcome to S&S, Your Royal Highness."

Over her two-day trip, the Duchess told me things she should not have told anyone. She seemed to feel isolated and alone. At the start of the party in the Rainbow Room, she took me aside and said, "John, I am exhausted, who are all these people?" I told her that everyone in the room would contribute to the success of her books. She said, "Right." She pulled her jacket tight and waded into the crowd. She spent two hours working hard, and she talked to every single guest; they never knew she was exhausted. She was near collapse when we left.

She departed the next day. The bill arrived from the hotel. Oh no. The room service charge was four times the lodging; she had entertained some friends. I had a third round of negotiations with the hotel manager.

The books were a success. We did two more and there was an animated TV series and some plush toys. Things were mostly smooth, though the press continually tormented her. At one point, when she was frustrated with sales, she called me and said she didn't think we were working hard enough. That managed to set me off, and I ended up expressing myself with a certain amount of vigor. In my urge to be direct, I was clearly not her most humble and obedient servant. I hung up and my assistant came in, visibly shaken. "John, that was the Duchess of York, you can't speak to her that way!"

Connie gave birth to a baby girl and so did the Duchess. We exchanged Christmas cards while the kids grew up. As the years went by, the Duchess would call occasionally or stop in to ask publishing advice about various projects. One day, after I had not heard from her for a few years, Sarah called me at my Macmillan office in the Flatiron Building. There was lots of noise in the background, and I asked where she was. She said she was on the runway. I said, "At Kennedy?"

She said, "No silly, I'm in Bryant Park at the Red Dress Fashion Show, can you come by?" I said sure and asked when. "How about now?"

I had the next two hours free, and it was only fifteen minutes away, so I hung up and started walking. A new equerry met me in front of the tents at Bryant Park and whisked me in the back door, straight into the dressing room for the models. There were models in various stages of undress. There were models practicing walking in their constricting new dresses. There were models getting their makeup done. That is where I found Sarah, sitting in a chair with two people working on her face. She blew me an air kiss, and I grabbed a free stool. We chatted for a while, and she asked me if I would stay to watch her turn on the runway. I did, and I marveled that among all the skinny and exotic looking women, Sarah was clearly the star of the show. In her bright red dress and with her big mane of red hair, she strode down the runway like she owned the place.

Sarah lasted ten years as Her Royal Highness. She is still the Duchess of York. I lasted six years working at Simon & Schuster. I had six bosses in that time, including Dick for a year. I saw the famous Snyder temper leveled at others, but never at me. I saw how difficult he could be in the pursuit of publishing success, and why he always made the list of America's top ten toughest bosses.

He never had the promised first-year party for me, but he never fired me either.

The Budgie books were occasionally problematic over the years. Toward the end of my stay at S&S, there was an issue with merchandising rights. All the people who had worked on Budgie in the United Kingdom were gone by then. I wrote Dick a memo asking if I should just handle all Budgie matters globally. He sent me back the memo with a single line handwritten at the top: "I hate Budgie."

6.

Eloise

I WAS TOLD WHEN I STARTED AT SIMON & SCHUSTER THAT THERE
was nothing to be gained by talking to Kay Thompson; I would
guess Dick was as fond of Kay as he was of Budgie. Kay was a
famous singer and actress and a vocal coach for Lena Horne and
Frank Sinatra. She sang in *Funny Face* with Audrey Hepburn and
Fred Astaire. She was the highest paid nightclub act in the world.
And in 1955, two years before I was born, she wrote "a book for
precocious grown-ups" called *Eloise*. Kay lived and worked at the
Plaza Hotel for a time, and it was rumored that the character Eloise
was based on Kay's goddaughter, Liza Minelli. Kay never confirmed
or denied that rumor, but she was dead certain that the book was
for adults, not children.

Simon & Schuster saw the book as a children's book because it
was a children's book. Years after Eloise was published, S&S created a children's book division. *Eloise* was moved from the adult
group and became the new division's lead title. Kay was apoplectic.
And she stayed that way. For years. Finally, in 1964, she became

so angry that she forced Simon & Schuster to take the recently published *Eloise* sequels off the market.

Hilary Knight illustrated all the *Eloise* books. He drew Eloise; he created the visual character. When he met Kay at her nightclub show, he was a young and struggling artist. Kay was a huge star, and she pushed him into giving her all his rights to the art of Eloise. I met Hilary when he began illustrating a new book for us; he came to me asking for help. He argued we would both be better off if the other *Eloise* books were back in print and if we could use the Eloise character more widely. It sounded entirely logical to me, so I agreed to take on the task. I never suspected it would take five years.

Kay was a hermit; she lived with Liza Minelli and never went out. Nor did she talk on the phone, at least not to anyone I could find. She did, on rare occasion, respond to letters. Those letters sometimes encouraged us, but eventually one would arrive containing the word no. Hilary persisted in his arguments, and we looked at the legal options. We determined that Hilary had no power, but S&S did have the rights to publish her other books, even over the author's objection. And so my letters to Kay started again, this time with a firmer tone.

Then Donald Trump bought the Plaza.

He and Ivana were constantly in the news, talking about their planned renovations, and how they would return the hotel to its former glory. Ivana loved Eloise and decided they would have an Eloise suite, with drawings of Eloise on the walls. The Trump organization got in touch with us, and we explained the situation with Kay and the rights to Eloise. They would need Kay's approval. Good luck with that.

A few weeks later a story ran in the *New York Post*. Ivana was seen at lunch with the elusive Kay Thompson. Shortly after that the Trump organization informed us that Ivana had gotten Kay to agree to the concept of the Eloise suite. The Trumps decided to gear up their *Eloise* branding, and we got a call asking us for a special edition of the book. They wanted it in a cloth slipcover, with an inlaid piece of art and, of course, lots of gaudy bright gold foil. *Eloise*, Trump style. My job was to get Kay's approval.

Remarkably, Kay was bewitched by Ivana and, after some back and forth, agreed to go forward with the special edition. We priced it and told the Trump organization what it would cost them. That started a long negotiation. The Trumps couldn't get the book anywhere else, so we decided not to budge on the price. A few days later my phone rang, and it was the Donald himself. He battered away at me for several minutes explaining how much money he was making for us, and how great his work at the hotel was going to be for us. I was unmoved. He did not slow down, and I began to wonder why this big-time real estate guy was working so hard to get a price. It wasn't a building; it was a book. Then it dawned on me. Perhaps he had told his staff that he would get us to come down in price; that he would succeed where they had failed. I interrupted his monologue and suggested that, if they were that committed to the book, we would take two cents off the price. He said, "We have a deal" and hung up.

Kay fell out of love with Ivana. We had the new Trump edition ready to print, and Kay directed us to stop it. The Trumps were pissed. Hilary was pissed. Kay was pissed. Finally, I decided to go ahead with the book. It seemed to me that Hilary should have the right to earn some money from his work, and that Kay had been giving approvals and then retracting them for years. Perhaps she was toying with us for sport. We sold the Trumps lots of copies of the new edition, and they went on sale in the Plaza gift shop. If you booked a fancy suite in the Plaza, you got one for free. S&S republished the *Eloise* sequels the following year, and they are still available today. Hilary was ecstatic. Kay was unhappy about all of it, though she didn't seem to mind the higher royalty payments. After we put the Trump edition on sale, she stopped writing me, but she did write a letter of complaint to Dick Snyder calling me "the reprehensible Mr. Sargent." Dick loved it.

7·

The President Builds a House

A LAN BENJAMIN APPEARED TO BE NERVOUS. HE SAT IN MY office and described a book he wanted to publish. Alan was a man of faith, and he had devoted a good part of his life to helping the homeless and the hungry. He was also our best editor. He explained to me that he wanted to do a nonfiction picture book for young children, illustrated with photographs, about Habitat for Humanity. Former president Jimmy Carter had just agreed to spend a week building houses with them, houses for people who could not afford a home otherwise. The new homeowners would work with the Habitat volunteers, and Alan thought it would make a great book. I thought it sounded like a terrible idea. He fidgeted a bit and told me that he not only wanted to do the book, but he wanted to give Habitat all the profits.

That sounded like an even worse idea. Simon & Schuster was all about the profits. Alan was firm that he wanted to do the project though and feeling that the cause was worthy, I relented. Shortly after we signed up the book, Jimmy Carter agreed to write the foreword. At least now we could use *The President Builds a House* as the title, and we could put his name on the cover.

Alan poured himself into the project. Habitat loved the book, and so did President Carter. I had some brief conversations with Millard Fuller, the founder and president of Habitat, and came to admire him and the organization. When they announced another Jimmy Carter work week in Milwaukee the following spring, Connie and I signed up.

The Jimmy Carter Work Week happened every year going forward. Primarily a publicity gambit, Habitat built houses in a week, from foundation to occupancy, landscaping included. In Milwaukee they planned to build six of them, each a two-story house that would blend in with the other houses in the neighborhood. President Carter, with his wife Rosalynn, would work on one of the houses. Connie and I would be working on the house next door. At the time, Connie and I were newly married, and we both had jobs with two weeks of vacation a year. Shortly before we arrived, we discovered we would be spending one of those weeks sleeping separately, her in the Habitat women's dorm and me in the men's dorm. It was not happy news.

Then it got worse. We discovered each day would begin with a prayer breakfast. I don't pray much, nor do I eat breakfast. On the first morning, as we gathered in the big tent for prayer and food, the sky opened. It rained hard all day; work was impossible. Now we would have to build a two-story house in five days instead of six.

The second day dawned clear; we were in the breakfast tent long before the sun cleared the horizon. We worked long into the night, with one fifteen-minute break for lunch. As it turned out, it is not easy to build a house in five days. President Carter worked as hard as anyone. You could tell the guys who knew what they were doing by their tool belts and hammers. The president had a well-worn hammer, and he knew how to swing it. I, on the other hand, had only rudimentary carpentry skills, but I had stamina and a good attitude. I spent a lot of time putting on the roof; shingles are not overly complex. I also spent lots of time unloading the constant stream of trucks that brought us materials every day, pure manual labor. The hours kept getting longer as it became clear how far behind we were. President Carter was adamant that we all finish on time. By the third night I stopped getting undressed; I just fell into my cot when the work was done.

It will not surprise you to hear that the most talented workers were assigned to the president's house. Also, when supplies ran low, the president's house got what it needed. This was as it should be; after all, the TV crews were not filming the Connie and John house. One day, while he was talking to the press, I had a chance to chat with President Carter about the book. Nice guy, but all business. That night, work on his house stopped a bit early as President Carter went to a press event in town. We worked on into the night. Too late, we realized we would run out of 2x4s, and if we didn't get more, we would fall further behind.

I had an idea about where I might find some. I went next door to the Carter house and discovered an impressive stash of extra lumber. I managed, quite easily, to convince myself that we needed the wood a hell of a lot more than they did. I loaded a short stack of 2x4s onto each shoulder. As I was walking through the living room, there was a commotion at the front door. A secret service agent came in, followed by President Carter. He was coming back to check on the progress of his house after attending a Habitat fundraising dinner. Admiring his work ethic, I gave him a cheerful hello. He gave me a stone stare. "What do you think you are doing with that wood?" I explained how far behind we were; he was having none of it. He made me put the wood back. He never smiled, not even a little. In a few short words he managed to fully express his displeasure with me and my actions.

We finished our house in a stunning flurry of subcontractors and supplies. As part of the program, we had worked the whole week side by side with the guy who would own the house when we were done. He was a good man, even if he was occasionally a bit picky about my workmanship. Seeing him and his wife looking at their completed house on the last day made every bit of the work, and the dorm living, worthwhile.

Years later we would publish President Carter's *White House Diary* at Macmillan, and I had dinner with him. I got the big smile and the charm that night. When I reminded him about my transgression in Milwaukee, he didn't seem to hold a grudge. But he didn't laugh about it either.

8.

I'll Meet You at the Top of the Coconut Tree

SOME BOOKS, LIKE THE HABITAT BOOK, WE PUBLISHED TO DO good in the world. Most books we published to make money. On occasion, a book came along that allowed us to do a lot of both. The first time I saw *Chicka Chicka Boom Boom* I saw it entirely, all in one glance. The original art for the book was spread out on a conference room table at S&S, and all the astonishing colors were even brighter than in its final printed form. I had an immediate sense of wonder, that rare moment when you see something new, something entirely different. And the text seemed magical to me. It was written more in syllables than in words, and the rhyming syllables, when read aloud, forced a sort of melody. If you read "A told B and B told C, I'll meet you at the top of the coconut tree," you will feel a certain lilt in the word coconut.

We knew we had something remarkable, but that didn't make it easy. The printing of the saturated colors was vexing and took longer than we hoped. Off press at last, with great gusto we launched our prize into the world. It was greeted with muted curiosity. We were shocked by the tepid response. Barnes & Noble passed on the book entirely. They refused to buy a single copy.

Our marketing director, Ken Geist, and I were flabbergasted, and we decided it was an unacceptable result. The next day we took the rare step of intervening directly with the buyers at B&N. Maureen Golden and Michael Cavanaugh, the head of merchandising and head buyer respectively, were pals, and they agreed that I could come down and give them a pitch. I delivered what I thought was a brilliant presentation. They were underwhelmed by my efforts and again refused to buy the book.

Thankfully, there were pockets of enthusiasm in the market. The book started to sell on the West Coast; children's booksellers, teachers, and librarians began to believe. Ken and I knew how powerful the book could be. We decided we could not accept defeat at B&N and that it was time for Plan B. The problem was—we had no Plan B. There was no way around Maureen and Michael, and they had been abundantly clear with us. With a touch of desperation, Ken suggested we should grow beards and refuse to shave them until B&N bought the book.

In 1989, most men working in corporations did not sport beards in the workplace. At Simon & Schuster in particular, and in publishing in general, it was suits and ties, no beards, no tattoos, no piercings. Occasionally men let their hair grow a little long, but a ponytail put you on the wild side. Ken's idea was brilliant or stupid; we were not sure which. But really, how could Maureen and Michael resist that level of commitment, and all that hair?

I penned a note to them explaining our intent and resolve. I asked them to reconsider and pointed out that our careers were now likely in their hands. Five days of stubble later I got their response: no dice. Undaunted, Ken and I continued to put our razors aside.

At the end of the second week, we took a Polaroid of ourselves and sent it to them with a note. We pointed out what was obvious, that we looked bad, and couldn't they please help? Again, no dice. The next week we sent another picture and a wordy complaint about the itchiness. No response. Ken and I got more elaborate with the weekly pictures, now always including the book with the beards. We went to sales conference in Florida and sent a picture of us in the pool wearing sunglasses, holding the book. "Do you have any idea how hot these beards are?"

Christmas season came, and very early one morning Ken and I went out into Rockefeller Center with a case of books. We put a copy in the hands of all the angel statues by the ice rink. "Even the Angels want these guys to shave." Silence from B&N.

The book was working well now, but it lacked the critical momentum it needed. The next week I wrote an impassioned letter, no pictures. "I am miserable. I hate this damn beard. My wife hates it, too, and it is impacting my love life. Please." The words had no more power than the pictures.

The next week, I went to a fancy fundraiser and sat at the head table with Dick Snyder. At the end of the dinner, Dick took me aside and asked if I was having an affair. Shocked, I responded, "Of course not, and why in the hell would you ask me that?"

He responded, "That is the only reason a guy your age would grow a beard." I explained that I was only growing the beard to sell more books for him and told him the story. He was not amused, not at all. "Lose the beard and lose it now."

Ken and I decided we would risk Dick's wrath and give it one more shot. The next day we brought razors to work, and we each shaved half our beards: he took off his right side, I took off my left. We took a last photo, two guys with one beard between them. I wrote a final appeal, and we sent it off to B&N. The next day we received our final rejection in return. We were dejected and, in all honesty, angry.

Later that week Maureen called; would I be available to join her and Michael for lunch? I arrived at the restaurant, clean shaven, and found them in high good humor. They delighted in reviewing the pictures and the notes with me, laughing all the while. Finally, and with a bit of attitude, I asked if they liked our approach so much, why did they refuse to buy the book? With a big smile, Maureen said they were loving it so much they'd just wanted to see how far we would go. Then she told me that starting at the beginning of the Easter season, there would be an entire table dedicated to *Chicka Chicka Boom Boom* in the front of every Barnes & Noble store in America. And the tables would stay up through the entire spring season, at no cost to S&S.

For the next few decades, whenever I shopped at Barnes & Noble, I would go into the children's section looking for my old friend. *Chicka Chicka Boom Boom* was always there. Over the years, it became one of the books I was proudest of, and a sort of talisman of my years in children's publishing.

I was happy working in kid's books. But after a few years at S&S, even after the success of *Chicka Chicka Boom Boom*, I could feel a sense of greater career ambition, a sense that work for me would need to be more than publishing books for young readers. There were other types of books to publish and there were other ways to accomplish more in the world. I found myself thinking, "What's next?"

9.

A Road Not Taken

WILLIAM SHEA WAS A POWERBROKER. IN 1958, AFTER THE Dodgers and the Giants left New York for California, Mayor Robert Wagner asked him to bring a National League team back to the city. Shea decided to launch the Continental League, and he got Branch Rickey to help him do it. The ploy worked, and in response, the National League agreed to expand. The New York Mets were born, and when they built a new stadium, they named it in honor of Bill. He also helped bring New York the Nets and the Islanders, and he was a force in street-level New York City politics. I was a small fry, and just looking for advice, but Mr. Shea agreed to see me.

I was thirty-one years old at the time, well started on a career in publishing, but wondering if I should try something new. I realized that if I was going to shift gears, now would be the time. I spent an afternoon on a mountaintop, thinking. By the time the sun went down, I knew if I was going to do something else it would be politics, and that I should at least explore the possibilities. I explained all this to Bill Shea, sitting in front of his massive desk at the Shea Gould law firm.

His response surprised me. "Why in the hell would you want to go into politics? It was a great job ten years ago, now it is crap." He explained why, and then kept explaining until his enthusiasm for the subject made it sound interesting. We jawed back and forth; he seemed to be enjoying himself. Then without preamble he picked up his phone, glanced straight at me, and placed a call. "Hi Jimmy." A pause. "Jimmy, I'm going to send you a kid, a good guy." A pause. "Don't worry, show him everything." A pause. "Yes, Jimmy, everything, the kid can know everything, I'm vouching for him." A pause. "OK. OK. Thanks, Jimmy."

Shea hung up, wrote an address on a card, and handed it to me. "Be at that address tomorrow night at 7:00. It's the Westside Democratic Club; ask for Jim McManus."

Jim was the last of New York's neighborhood political bosses. He would be the district leader (an elected position) in Hell's Kitchen for fifty-four years. He ran the Westside Democratic Club, which had started operating in 1892. Jim's great-uncle took it over in 1905, and it had been run by a member of the McManus family ever since. It was often referred to as the McManus Democratic Club. Jim ran a funeral parlor as a side job, and he lived down the block. The club phone rang in his apartment. Jim described the work of the club to the *New York Times* in 2017: "In the old days you could get people jobs, take care of their problems, help them with their daily lives." The people were mostly poor immigrant Irish families.

I knew none of this the next night when I left work at Rockefeller Center and walked west into Hell's Kitchen. I arrived at the club and stepped into a sort of time warp. Tammany Hall-style retail politics was still the game at the club, and a game played well.

It was a small place, an informal apartment on a steady decline toward shabby. The first thing I learned was that Jim was Jimmy.

The second thing I learned was that we were open for business for our constituents on Monday and Thursday nights, and I was expected to be there both nights, every week. I agreed, and Jimmy put me to work.

A Democratic Club works on a simple concept. The club helps you with your problems, and you, in exchange, show up when the club needs you, push the club's candidates, and vote for whomever the club endorses. Two nights a week Jimmy would sit in his office and a steady stream of Hell's Kitchen residents would file through asking for help. It was mostly small stuff, like traffic tickets, job interviews, school applications, a loan, a subsidized apartment. It felt a lot like *The Godfather* but without the violence. Jimmy would say, "I'm still collecting on favors that were done twenty years ago by my father, and fifty years ago by my great-uncle."

I had a seat outside of Jimmy's office and helped smooth the flow of people and favors. Mostly I was a lackey, doing odd jobs on demand. In my first week, Senator Daniel Patrick Moynihan called. He was coming to the city for a surprise visit in two days and needed the hall packed with enthusiastic supporters. We started calling constituents. We asked them to show up and maybe to bring a sign. But it wasn't really asking, if you know what I mean.

After the first few weeks, Jimmy occasionally asked me to sit in the office with him. At other times, he grabbed me as he was leaving and took me to the diner down the street. He nursed a cup of coffee, and I got lessons in New York politics. Mario Cuomo was governor then (our guy), Ed Koch was mayor (not our guy), and the fireworks between them were constant. Jimmy was usually somehow in the mix, and he explained what was happening.

As the weeks passed, my jobs at the club got a bit more edgy. One night I found myself handing a manila envelope through a car window. You can tell when an envelope contains a stack of cash. No one ever said what the money was for, and I never questioned it.

Toward the end of my time at the club I was sitting in Jimmy's office, a slow night. A small old man came in, signs of a tough life on his face. He was a long-standing bartender in the neighborhood and for years he had a one-bedroom apartment over the bar. He told us that when the bar closed, he was fired, and they threw him out of the apartment. Jimmy just listened, full of compassion. When the guy finished, Jimmy said there was a rent-subsidized apartment building that had just been completed, and he instructed the bar-keep to get himself into next week's lottery for an apartment. They exchanged some information and the guy left. Jimmy got on the phone to arrange a favorable outcome. Two weeks later the bar-keep was back, close to tears. Jimmy asked what happened. The guy said he had filled the form out in pencil, but it was required to be in ink, so they had rejected his form and now the lottery was over. Jimmy was very gentle. He told him there must have been a mistake, and would he please come back and see us on Thursday?

The guy left the office, and he took all of Jimmy's gentleness with him. Jimmy picked up the phone and dialed. With a hard voice: "My guy didn't get an apartment." And then, after a pause, "That is complete bullshit. Now you listen to me. My guy got a lottery number last week, and it was a low number, you understand?" When he hung up, I asked the obvious question: If there was a lottery last week, didn't someone else already have the apartment? Jimmy explained that the developers, architects, and others who built the housing always skimmed a few of the subsidized apartments for themselves, and then flipped them for cash. The apartments were picked in the order of the numbers drawn in the lottery; low numbers meant better apartments. Guess who got the low numbers.

On Thursday I waited for the barkeep. The guy bounced in, the slouch was gone, and he had a smile like the sun. "I got it, Mr. McManus, I got one of the best apartments in the place!" Jimmy congratulated him and said he was glad it had all worked out.

Many years later I read a quote from Jimmy: "I wouldn't ever do anything for money that I wouldn't do for nothing." I knew that to be true.

One day, early in my shift, Jimmy asked me to join him at the diner. This was something new, and as we walked down the street, I sensed it was business, not a chat. He got his coffee, looked me in the eye, and said, "It is time for you to run." Surprised, I just nodded. "We are going to put you on the City Council. You are gonna have to stand at some subway stations. You're gonna have to kiss some babies and shake some hands. But you will win, I can guarantee that. In the future, I think you can make it at the national level, and we will help."

He let me sit there quietly. He sipped coffee, I thought. After a minute I said, "I can't do it, Jimmy." It was his turn to be surprised, and he asked why not. I explained that it was too difficult for me, that I had problems with what we did and how we did it.

He said, "Look. The fix is in. Everywhere in New York the fix is in for the rich people. We put the fix in, but for the people who really need it." I told him I knew that; I had seen it with my own eyes over the months. But that didn't mean I was comfortable with it. I also saw us supporting politicians and programs we didn't like simply because that's how the system works. The system felt wrong to me, corrupted somehow. I told him I had enormous respect for him and what he did, but that I couldn't do it. I promised I would always send a check in those little envelopes we mailed out. I did for years, and we stayed in touch until my life in publishing and a growing family pulled me in other directions.

After Jimmy died a few years ago, I saw a quote about him that felt just right. "In the old days we used to vote the graveyards," Mr. McManus's election lawyer observed. "Jim is a reformer; he voted the funeral parlor."

10.

Kyle's Courage

S HORTLY AFTER MY SIDE JOB IN POLITICS CAME TO AN END, Connie and I had a baby girl named Kyle. Dick Snyder sent her a huge stuffed bear, a nice touch from a tough guy. Kyle was a delight, particularly at bedtime. It was magic to feel her snuggled up beside me as we shared the books I was publishing. Many were the nights that started with "A told B and B told C." Kyle loved books from the start, and she would go on to be an enthusiastic focus group of one for the rest of my years in publishing. After she was born, I tried to get home every night for dinner. I was usually successful, but weeknights were always too short. On the weekends, there was time to be together.

One weekend, when she was about four, Kyle decided we needed to go shopping for a new jigsaw puzzle. She was always great company, it was a fine summer morning, and we headed to a mall in high spirits. We walked into the toy store, and the trouble started quickly. I pointed to the 150-piece puzzles and asked which one she would like. She pointed to a 1,000-piece puzzle and told me that was what we should buy. I explained that it would be too difficult for us to put together. She explained that what mattered most was the picture. Both good arguments, soundly based in logic.

But as the discussion continued it became an argument, and then a test of wills. She ended up in a tantrum, using her outside voice. Our fellow customers were getting an earful, and I was embarrassed. She became more difficult, I became angry. Finally, I just dragged her out into the parking lot; she was screaming for all she was worth. We sat on a bench. As she kept ranting about the puzzle, my anger stayed with me. Unable to stop her, or convince her, I decided to use the guy's way: silence. I told her that until she could be reasonable, I was not going to talk to her. She continued to express her frustration in no uncertain terms; I sat silently, staring straight ahead. She asked me a question; I remained silent, still staring straight ahead. She got madder, more animated; I did not move or speak.

I sensed motion beside me and through the corner of my eye I saw her stand and climb onto the bench. She stood beside me, her head now even with mine. She reached over, grabbed my chin, and yanked my head around so she could look me straight in the eye, "You. Will. Talk. To. Me." Her eyes were wide, her skin mottled from all the crying. Her face was fierce, etched with resolve and determination. I knew I was beaten. I suggested we go home. We loaded into the car, I said something, and she replied. We rode in silence, but a different silence. Though I was still mad, I thought about how much a guy could learn from a four-year-old. I marveled at her courage and determination.

She can still talk a blue streak; I am sometimes too silent. Over time, her life has tested her in ways that would have derailed me. But her grit, seen first on a summer morning in a shopping mall parking lot, has always been there.

11.

Green Tigers and S. T. Garne

W E HAD DONE WELL OVER MY FIRST FOUR YEARS AT SIMON & Schuster, but steadily increasing profits were proving elusive. Buying more books wouldn't solve the problem, but buying a company might. And thus, I found myself in the back aisle of a convention center, wandering through the small publisher booths, looking for a company to buy. Rounding a corner, I was startled to see two green tigers.

I stopped to admire the beasts, and the books displayed on the table between them. I learned that the tigers were from an antique carousel, and that their yellow eyes were glass. I learned the publisher was Green Tiger Press, and that they published *Good Dog Carl*, a hugely popular wordless picture book. Though I continued to walk the aisles, I sensed that I had found what I was looking for.

Green Tiger Press was based in San Diego. It had been purchased a few years before by a retired guy from the forklift business named Jerry Macchia. I called him the next week, and by chance he had decided publishing was not for him. He was delighted to get my call. He sent me some figures, and we agreed on a price. The S&S lawyers got busy with a contract to buy the assets, and I went to see Dick Snyder for approval. Dick gave me some advice. "You can buy a big company and run it wherever you like. If you buy a small company, you need it to be local, or you have to fold it in." He approved the acquisition, but my plans to leave Green Tiger as an independent company in San Diego were dead on arrival.

We bought the company, and I flew out to San Diego to load some trucks and close up shop. It was a sad day. From the offices you could tell it had been a vibrant place. Now it felt vacated, ghostly quiet. While we were packing files and artifacts, some of the former employees stopped by. Jerry had told them about selling the company only after the transaction was complete, so they were fired the day before I arrived. And Jerry had decided to do it on a conference call. Their wounds were fresh, and they told me in no uncertain terms what they thought of me, and of the corporation I worked for. On the flight home I kept thinking of them, and I decided I would stick to buying books, not companies, in the future.

Back in New York, the books of Green Tiger Press prospered; our profits went up as planned. One of the green tigers stood guard in our lobby, the other crouched in the rafters at the warehouse, keeping watch over the books. Most of the sales continued to come from Sandra Day's *Good Dog Carl* and a series of books by Cooper Edens.

While I was in San Diego, I had met with Sandra. I discovered her real name was not Day, and that she had previously owned part of the company. She also told me that Cooper Edens had been the editorial director, as well as being a Green Tiger author and illustrator. Cooper Edens wasn't his real name either.

My job continued to grow at seriously corporate S&S, but I often thought back to the small company in San Diego, where the people who published the books also wrote and illustrated them.

The next winter, in the Caribbean, I found a remarkable local artist named Lisa Etre. She painted stills of island life, bounded by intricate borders. I thought that, given a chance, she could illustrate a counting book for preschool kids. Remembering the Green Tiger tradition, I decided to try my hand at writing it. I tasked myself with creating scenes for Lisa to draw and writing a text in rhyming couplets that would add to the atmospherics.

I set to work. The manuscript was only eighty-one words, and I labored over every syllable. Then came the tricky part: I had to find out if my work was any good. And if it was good, I had to find a way to publish it. I was certain I didn't want the book published if it wasn't worthy. I was equally certain no one should know I was involved.

In those days, we still accepted unsolicited manuscripts from the general public. This allowed us to learn, among many other things, that lots of people write kids' books about their cats, illustrated with Polaroids. We got hundreds of manuscripts a week and, as the publisher, I had a steady flow across my desk. I sent them on to various editors in batches, but in four years we had never found anything to publish. The week after I finished my two-page manuscript, I slipped it into a stack of unsolicited manuscripts and sent them down the hall to Alan Benjamin, the guy who had brought in the Habitat project.

A few days later Alan stuck his head into my office. He said, "You are not going to believe this, but I found something in that slush you sent me. I want to publish it." I held my breath as he continued, "The only problem is the manuscript has no contact information for the author. Did you save the envelope from a guy named S. T. Garne?"

I tried to look puzzled and assured him I would look for the envelope, "It must be here somewhere."

The next morning Alan stopped by. I asked him to close the door and take a seat. He gave me a raised eyebrow and sat down warily. I swore him to secrecy, and he solemnly agreed that he would never speak of whatever I told him. I revealed that I was S. T. Garne.

We spent the next hour plotting how to publish the book and keep the secret. Garne needed a persona, and a reason to be unreachable. We decided to make him a marine biologist, a career I had hoped for back in high school. It was a job that required long trips to remote places, and that would be handy. The mechanics of the deal were complicated. I wrote the book for the company, and thus there would be no royalties, but we needed an author contract. We debated using a fake social security number. We filled out the author questionnaire. When we had decided on the way forward, I told him that I had an illustrator in mind for the book. I gave him Lisa's address.

Alan liked Lisa's work, and having been an art director, he took over the creative process. We celebrated alone in a conference room when Lisa's art arrived. Alan chose the jacket art and the title, *One White Sail*. The book was presented at sales conference without fanfare, just another title on the list. When we published *One White Sail* it got a starred review. The critic understood exactly what we were trying to do; reading his explanation was remarkably gratifying. The reviews kept coming, the sales were surprisingly good, and we were selected for a textbook anthology. The publicity and marketing folks clamored for Garne; there was demand for author appearances in stores and libraries. Alan deflected and never told a soul.

Many months later Ken Geist strolled into my office looking pleased with himself. He slouched back in his chair. He said, "I know." Genuinely puzzled, I asked him what he was talking about. He just sat there grinning. Then he said, "I figured it out. S T G A R N E spells Sargent."

After I left S&S, I wrote another book, which was published by Harcourt. It didn't do quite as well. Years later Roger Priddy and

I wrote a book together; it was a Priddy Garne good book. It was fantastically fun, but the book didn't sell. As I got increasingly busy, S. T. retired.

In the years ahead I stuck with the lesson I learned at Green Tiger Press. At Macmillan, we grew our business primarily by finding talented people and starting companies, not buying them. But before going to Macmillan, I spent the next three years at Dorling Kindersley (DK), where I learned a lot about untraditional publishing. Among other things, I learned about design, about creating software, and about product marketing. I learned that books about gardening are hugely popular in the United Kingdom, and books about sex are hugely popular in America. And most interesting of all, I learned about a new way of selling books.

12.

The DK Family Library

W E COULD HEAR THE CROWD RUSTLING FROM OUR ASSIGNED spot behind the curtain. Roger Priddy and I had received our instructions: listen for your name, step around the curtain, and jog (do not run, do not walk) to the other side of the stage. Be sure to constantly smile and wave to the audience.

Suddenly all the lights went out and a booming voice filled the dark space, "Ladies and gentlemen, it is my great pleasure to introduce you tonight to the man responsible for all of Dorling Kindersley's business in the United States. He is a member of Peter Kindersley's executive board. He has flown all the way from New York City to be with you. Please welcome . . . JOOOHHN SARGENT!" That was the cue, so I stepped around the curtain. I was instantly blinded by a spotlight. The crowd was on their feet and the volume of their voices was overwhelming. For a second, I was a deer in the headlights. Then I started my jog across the massive stage, waving and smiling as I had been told to. The full-throated cheering of 1,200 people continued for my entire journey.

Roger was up next, and he got the same treatment. Welcome to Vegas.

It was 1994, and we were at the annual gathering of the Dorling Kindersley Family Library. The people gathered here were independent operators who ran small businesses selling DK products in their home communities. DKFL was a multilevel marketing organization like Avon, Tupperware, or Mary Kay. The folks had paid their own way to Las Vegas to hear about new products, to iron out operational difficulties, and to give us feedback. But the real reason they were here was to be inspired. They wanted to hear from others like themselves, and from us. They were mostly women, and mostly moms. Almost all of them worked part time selling DK books to friends and neighbors in rural and small-town America. Many were evangelicals, and many homeschooled their kids. Our books had great educational value, and most of the DKFL people gathered in Las Vegas got a huge dose of self-esteem from enhancing education in their communities and earning a few bucks along the way.

All multilevel marketing organizations need a charismatic leader at the top. Peter Kindersley filled that role for DKFL. He was an unlikely candidate in personality and appearance, but he founded the company and invented DK design, so he fit the bill. The DKFL folks adored him at a level approaching worship. Peter was not scheduled to attend this conference, though; Roger and I had come to stand in for him. We did our best over the next two days to inspire the masses. They loved Roger's accent and his easy British charm, and the two of us had good chemistry on stage, but we were not Peter.

At the final session, we had a surprise for the gathered faithful. DKFL generally sold older DK titles that were no longer on the shelves at retail. In addition, they sold some second-tier titles that were available in stores. But they had long wanted to sell *Timelines of the Ancient World*, one of DK's biggest books. Before the meeting we had decided to pull the book from distribution in bookstores and give it to them to sell exclusively, something we had never done with a bestseller before. Now we would announce it. Alan Luce, who ran DKFL, announced the book with his booming-voice-in-the-dark energy. Then a spotlight came on, pointed upward, and with confetti and a soundtrack, a twenty-foot-tall mockup of the book was lowered slowly from the ceiling. The crowd went into an ecstatic frenzy.

Alan finally restored order, and the presentations continued. It was early December, and as Alan talked about the great books they would have to sell, a Santa Claus character came out and gave him the books, one by one, out of a large sack. Alan thanked Santa for each new offering as the books flashed up on the huge screen. The last book presented, now for the second time, was *Timelines of the Ancient World*. Santa handed a copy to Alan, and the crowd roared again. Then Santa stepped back, faced the crowd, and ripped off his hat and beard. It was Peter Kindersley. Bedlam. The Beatles came to New York. Kindersley came to Vegas.

But DKFL never became the major distribution network Peter Kindersley envisioned. A few years later it collapsed. But in those early years Peter had created a new way to distribute books, no easy feat. Unknown to us at the time, not so far from the city of sin, another guy was hard at work on a different distribution concept. His would be more successful.

13.

Thinking Big

Tony Schulte was a high-level Random House executive turned headhunter. He called me in 1995, the week before a book convention, and suggested I meet a bright young guy who was starting a new business. Tony generally offered good advice, so I agreed without hesitation. When I arrived in Washington, DC, the next week, I discovered with some irritation that the meeting was scheduled at an offsite location. I almost skipped it, but I remembered Tony's enthusiasm, so at the appointed hour I made my way to a hotel on the far side of Georgetown.

I expected to meet in a conference room and was surprised when the front desk directed me to a hotel room instead. And it was a room, not a suite. Two queen beds. I was greeted by three young men in company T-shirts and baseball caps. Two were standing between the beds. The third one was by the door. He stuck his hand out. "Hi, I'm Jeff Bezos."

He told me about a new company he was launching. Judging by the T-shirts and hats, it was going to be called Amazon. The business plans were laid out on the bed closest to the door, and over the next half hour he walked me through them. His enthusiasm was infectious. He was clearly enormously intelligent. He had a nerdy sort of charm and a distressing honk of a laugh.

I was running DK's US business at the time. We published illustrated nonfiction, with a very distinctive graphic look. I asked Jeff if it would make sense for us to have a store within his store. He loved the idea, and we discussed how we might do it. Eventually I suggested that DK should design it, and I watched his expression change. Outside involvement on his website was clearly a step too far. At the end of the meeting, as we walked the two short steps to the door, Jeff asked for my commitment to sell every title we had on Amazon. He said he would be happy to pay our standard terms of sale.[3]

I liked him, and after a moment's thought, I agreed to sell him our whole catalogue. We shook hands. That was the start of an annual ritual; year in and year out we would always meet somewhere and set aside an hour to discuss Amazon's expansion plans. His ambition was relentless. In my last year at DK, and through much of my time at Macmillan, I continually underestimated it.

In the early years, as Amazon grew, Jeff assigned the day-to-day work with publishers to extremely smart and aggressive executives, usually women, usually graduates of Microsoft. They generally stayed for a year or two before being promoted. Every year I flew out to Seattle to meet with the current person in charge.

The Amazon offices moved constantly, it seemed, but they were consistently spartan. The desks were all made from doors. The dress code was extremely casual. The tempo was aggressive. After a while you knew what to expect. One year, after my move to Macmillan, I arrived and was shown down a hall to the office

---

3   His desire to sell our books never changed, but his happiness with our standard terms didn't last.

of the current head of publisher relations. It was eleven in the morning; I was fresh off the early flight from New York. I walked into her office to discover she was in a skintight, bright red dress, with a plunging neckline and makeup to match. I said something intelligent, like "Wow."

She laughed. "I'm dressed for tonight. I'm going to a party, and I am hunting for a husband." She told me years later that she had indeed found herself a husband that night. It was like that at Amazon. They were efficient, and they got what they set their sights on.

A few years later at our annual get-together, I had a serious bone to pick with Jeff. Amazon had always discounted heavily; it was one of the foundations of their business. But now the discounting had become incredibly aggressive, and they were in a price war with Walmart. In the previous months, the Amazon price on some books had reached 50 percent off; they were selling our books just below cost, and it was screwing up the market.

We had no power to determine what they charged for our books; the antitrust laws are clear on the topic. But I wanted to understand his thinking, so I said, "You buy the book for ten bucks, then you sell it for ten bucks, and meanwhile you are paying people and rent, building warehouses and investing in technology. That cannot work."

He smiled and said, "Trust me, it works." By this time, I knew that Jeff was smarter than me, smarter by a country mile. I told him that, and then I asked him to enlighten me on exactly how it worked. He laughed and told me again, "It works."

As we were walking out, I said, "OK, assuming it works, how long can you keep doing it?"

He replied, "Forever."

It would take me some time to see it. Books were only the first act of the play. Amazon had incredible customer loyalty from the start, and he knew he would eventually be selling everything, not just books. He was buying a new lifelong customer for all the products Amazon would sell in the future, by selling them a book for no profit today.

Several years later, a printed invitation arrived on my desk from Amazon. This was something new. Jeff was coming to town, and he wanted to talk to publishers, so much so that he was buying dinner, an unheard-of expenditure. The Amazon account folks called to say it was important that I be there.

They chose a swell place. It was a large room with forty or fifty of us seated at big round tables. There was a lively buzz, and when dinner arrived the waiters came flowing out with individual plates covered with silver domes. They got in position around the tables and then, in a single motion, they lifted the domes and placed the plates. Fancy stuff. I was slightly alarmed that I didn't get a silver dome, or a plate. No food at all. Everyone started eating, and I looked around, puzzled. Then I noticed a waiter coming out from the back. He had a single plate under a silver dome, and he was headed my way. The waiter stopped beside me, then with a flourish lifted the dome. On the plate was a McDonald's Quarter Pounder, still in its box, and a large order of fries. It was my favorite meal, delivered hot. Amazon always did believe in giving the customer what they want.

After dinner Jeff gave a presentation complete with slides. He showed us how the new Amazon recommendation engine would work using his latest passion, treehouses. The new engine would automatically recommend books Amazon thought you would like, given what books you had looked for previously. Flashy stuff in its day. And then we discovered the true purpose of the dinner. There was a new kid on the block, a company that wanted to house all the world's content, with a search engine to make that content accessible to everyone. Jeff wanted to make very clear to all of us that Amazon was our friend and that the new player, Google, was not.

That night, I tried the new Amazon recommendation engine by looking up Jeff's favorite books about treehouses. It worked. But then for the next decade or so, Amazon kept pushing treehouse books my way. I don't have any interest in treehouses. On the other hand, they did get it right with the Quarter Pounder.

* * *

More years passed, the early digital reading devices arrived, and Amazon entered the fray. They came to see us regularly with their strange device, and we offered blunt feedback. When Amazon came to New York to launch the Kindle, they realized at the last minute that they had no publisher quotes in their press material. They called me and asked if I could possibly give them a quote, and make it positive if not glowing? Yes, of course. I was naive.

The launch was a success. Amazon called and asked if Jeff could stop by for a chat on his way out of town. By then our annual get-togethers had stopped, so I perceived it as a "thank you for your help" sort of thing. He came to my office, and we talked about the launch, publishing, and Amazon. It was all very relaxed, a couple of guys leaning back in their chairs chewing the fat. And then suddenly he was leaning forward, arms on the table, fully intense. He explained to me that he was completely sure the future of digital books was subscription. We should figure out the model and start. I disagreed. Yes, it would be good for Amazon, and it might even be good for publishers, but there was no way a subscription model would benefit the vast majority of authors. If there was any question, all you had to do was look at what subscription was doing to the music business. We went back and forth with increasing tension. He said it was something we had to do. I finally said, "Macmillan will do subscription over my dead body." That stopped the conversation.

In the years ahead, new Amazon execs would look at me knowingly and say, "I know you don't like subscription models, but . . . "

In early 2010, we had a heated battle with Amazon, and I was the public face for Macmillan. A few years later, *Vanity Fair* did their usual ranking of the most powerful people in media, and Jeff landed in the top five. There was a sidebar in the story that was headlined, "Thorn in His Side." The thorn was reported to be "Macmillan's John Sargent." By then Amazon was our largest customer and only getting bigger. I called Russ Grandinetti, an old Amazon hand whom I had worked with for years, and asked if he could set up a meeting with Jeff. I wanted five minutes, just enough time to make sure we were square. Russ responded the next day. Jeff did not want to see me for five minutes. But he did want to see me for an hour, and I should bring a big idea, a big idea that was good for Macmillan and good for Amazon. By this time, Jeff was one of the richest people in the world. His side gig was putting people into space, and for vacation he and the family rented a huge salvage vessel and pulled rockets off the ocean floor. What sort of idea would he consider "big"?

On the appointed day I landed in Seattle and drove straight to the new Amazon offices by Lake Union. I got to the meeting a few minutes late. There was a small group gathered in a conference room, and Jeff was sitting on the far side of the table, in the middle. There was an open seat opposite him, and he waved me into it. I had not seen Jeff in a few years, and he looked remarkably different. The slightly chubby cheeks were gone; his face was all angles now. His eyes were harder, and the bubbling enthusiasm was muted. Tremendous power can change people physically, and I saw it in Jeff.

We briefly discussed my status as a thorn. It got one of his signature laughs, and he said there had never been any hard feelings. Then he sat back, put his hands out, palms up, and said, "Let's hear your big idea." The others all looked at me expectantly. I braced myself and said, "My idea is based on the fact that Amazon sucks at marketing." This was met with a few hard stares and silence, which

I filled quickly. "In the beginning the site had a voice provided by the editors. Now you are a truly fantastic retailer, but you don't actually market the books for shit." Again, the stony faces.

Then Jeff broke into a big smile and said, "You're right, we have never been any good at marketing." People in the room, myself included, began to breathe again.

I laid out my idea for publisher-controlled marketing at Amazon in some detail. A lively discussion ensued. Jeff assigned people to follow up. As the hour reached its end, he sat back with a thoughtful expression. Then he said, "Congratulations, John, that is a big idea, and a good one."

There are moments in life when you simply have no respect for yourself. I had such a moment. I tried to keep a straight face, but I suspect there was a silly-looking grin. Jeff Bezos thought I had a big idea! I felt like I'd gotten an A in third grade. If I'd been a puppy, I would have been wagging my tail.

In the Amazon machine, the idea morphed into something else. It changed into something that was not good for Macmillan, and was not good for Amazon. Shortly thereafter, it was scrapped. In the years that followed, Jeff's ambition never slowed; his ideas just kept getting bigger.

PART III
Macmillan

St. Martin's Press, Macmillan, Holtzbrinck. Twenty-four years
at a company owned by one family. The goals I set were always
the same: #1, Grow faster than the competition. #2, Make a
good return for the Holtzbrinck family. #3, Have fun while doing
#1 and #2. In 2010, I added goal #4, Do less harm to the earth.
Thirteen years as an officer on the Board of the Association of
American Publishers.
The battles that defined the company, and me along with it.
Chasing what was right.

1996–2021

I.

Nicky

H E WAS A HANDSOME LITTLE DOG, BRIGHT EYED AND SURE OF himself. He came to me without hesitation, paused briefly at my feet, looked me over, and jumped into my lap. I scratched his ears and he settled in for the long haul. It was not the way most interviews for a CEO job start.

I was in London on a spring day in 1996 to interview for the top job at St. Martin's Press. Nicky Byam Shaw, who would be my boss, asked that we meet at his home in Kensington Park Gardens. It was a lovely old house, on a block of lovely old houses. I knocked on the door. The man who answered looked much like you would expect given his name and his house, a slender and elegant man with a silver mane of hair. I don't remember what suit he wore that day, but his impeccable suits were often hand-me-downs from his grandfather and father. Nicky would always assure me that good British tailoring and fine British wool could last forever.

He ushered me into a majestic living room with high ceilings and glass doors overlooking the garden out back. The inside walls were covered from floor to ceiling with oil paintings, mostly of Byam Shaws, or by Byam Shaws. I sat, Nicky perched on the arm of a chair, and Nicky's dog stretched out with me. In the afternoon sun we talked about business and books, a friendly chat more than an interview. I asked him at one point if he had trouble working for a German company. Macmillan Ltd, the company Nicky ran as managing director, had recently been acquired by the Holtzbrinck family, and I had considered what it would be like to work for Germans. Nicky told me his father had died in the war, and he remembered well the London Blitz. But these are different times, and these are different Germans, he said, and it does no good to live in the past. That put the issue to rest.

The next time I saw Nicky he was my boss, and he had come to New York for his twice-yearly visit. Like the interview in London, these visits were not normal meetings. We gathered around a table in my office, four or five executives. We sat and Nicky stood at the end of the table, his papers resting on a simple wooden podium built for that purpose. We all had the current financial statements in front of us, and Nicky asked questions. From nine in the morning until five at night he asked questions. And the questions were often odd, insightful, and thought provoking. He never sat. At some point around four he smacked his lips. "I say, might we have a little Madeira?" I discovered we had several bottles of the dry fortified wine stored in the back of a hallway closet for just this moment.

In London, Nicky hosted meetings of the Macmillan Ltd. board. Senior executives flew in from around the world. At lunch the conference table was set with fine linen, heavy silver, and vintage china. The meetings were formal, and minutes were reviewed and often commented on. This, after all, was the house of Macmillan, recently owned and operated by the former prime minister, Harold Macmillan, with whom Nicky had traveled the world.

In between the meetings in London and New York, there were genial phone calls. Nicky never let me off the hook, nor did he seek to have his way. He was forever curious, constantly trying to discover how I viewed things, from the balance sheet to an obscure novel. At times in business, he was ruthless, generally when he needed to be. But he cared deeply for the people of Macmillan. He hosted trips to the racetrack for retirees. He knew everyone's spouse and remembered all their children's names. After he retired, I got a note from Nicky. It was a list of all the employees he needed to be informed about should they die. Twenty years later, he still writes to their spouses and children to express his condolences and to say thank you.

After he left the company, he enrolled at Dartmouth, a sixty-six-year-old freshman. He didn't get grades and had no need to matriculate. What he wanted was the education. I rang him during his first semester, and he told me of a paper he was writing for his American history class. It was about a dock strike in the 1950s. He said it was fascinating work, but the associate professor was a bit leery of his questions in class. I asked how long his paper was. He replied that the assignment was ten pages, but he was on page 105 and still going. I pitied the poor young prof.

Over time I gradually learned things about Nicky. He was a school kid when his father, a thirty-five-year-old destroyer captain, died in the Battle of the Atlantic. He knew what the news would be when an officer knocked on their door; he had experience with these things. Some months before, his favorite uncle and godfather had come to the same end defending the Belgian canals, and Nicky had been with his grandmother when she got the dreaded orange telegram.

Nicky dropped out of school at age fourteen, joined the merchant marine, and served in the Navy during the Korean War (without distinction, he would claim). His financial questions were always odd because he had never learned business math from a textbook; instead, he discovered his own patterns and relationships between numbers. There was a lot to learn from him.

Now about the Madeira. Nicky had severe radiation burns from a cancer treatment gone wrong. It was extremely painful and made it impossible for him to sit. Remarkably, he never changed his travel schedule. When I asked him how he managed his annual trip to Japan, he showed me how he could hold himself above the seat with the seatbelt on for takeoffs and landings. And during the flight of course one could just stand in the galley. In the New York meetings, the Madeira, which I had always thought of as a sort of British mannerism, was an anesthetic. In all the years I worked with him, I never heard a complaint from Nicky about his own discomfort. He was sure sad when that dog died, though, and so was I.

Nicky was a legendary figure in British publishing, but he was always a professional manager, a behind-the-scenes guy, all competence and hard work and someone else can grab the spotlight, thank you very much. In the US offices, we also had a legend or two. One in particular wasn't the least bit behind the scenes. Roger Straus was never shy.

2.

Roger Straus

Roger Straus started Farrar, Straus and Giroux in 1946 and turned it into one of the world's great literary publishing houses, some say by the sheer magnitude of his personality. Dieter von Holtzbrinck bought FSG in 1994 with the promise to Roger that he could run it as he saw fit for as long as he liked. Roger was a magnificent man, large and brash. He wore ascots. He said things like "Fuck the peasants." He had stamps with an inkpad on his desk that he used to respond to correspondence. One said "Great moments in literature" and the other said "Fuck you very much."

Just before I started at St. Martin's Press in 1996, I called Roger and asked him to lunch. We had never met, and I wanted to propose that we work together on paperbacks of FSG's more commercial books. He said he would take me to the Union Square Café. From then on, whenever I needed to talk with Roger, I called him and asked him to take me to lunch. We ate at the Union Square Cafe, in the back corner. His table, table thirty-eight.

At the first lunch, I thanked Roger for saying nice things about me in the press when my appointment at SMP was announced. I noted that it was rare for him to be so free with compliments when talking with reporters. He replied, "Of course I said nice things; I used to have the hots for your grandmother."

Toward the end of lunch that day, Danny Meyer, the owner of Union Square Cafe, stopped by to pay his respects. Roger introduced us and said I would be starting soon at SMP. Danny politely asked if I was in editorial. Roger grabbed his arm, pulled him close, and said, "Danny, he runs the whole fucking thing." Danny offered me my own table at Gramercy Tavern on the spot. I had always wondered how these things worked. Now I knew, but Danny's place was too upscale for the likes of me.

When I was eventually given responsibility for all the Holtzbrinck book publishers in the United States, Roger continued to report directly to Dieter von Holtzbrinck, the owner in Germany. The FSG board meetings at the time were high theater. They took place in Roger's office, a windowed corner overlooking Union Square. Roger would describe the new FSG list and talk at length about his favorite books, often standing up to pull them from the shelves. There was champagne to celebrate the latest National Book Award or Nobel Prize. At the end there was a brief glance at the budget, with a few words about the figures.

Before one such occasion, Dieter asked me to prepare some extra analysis about FSG expenses. I scrambled to get it done and thus arrived at the meeting ten minutes late and breathless. I tried to ease quietly into the room, but Roger boomed out, "Ah, good. My warehouse man is here at last." Boardroom politics at the grandmaster level.

When Dieter retired, Roger reported to me. At least that's the way it looked on the organization chart. In reality we reached a sort of truce. He accepted the things I felt we had to do, and I accepted that he was right on everything else. We had our lunches. He was a gossip, and he told stories with a conspirator's flair. Interesting people stopped by his table to bask in a moment of his attention.

As the years flowed by, Roger began to slow down. It became clear that it was Jonathan Galassi's time to run the company. It wasn't an easy moment for any of us, but Roger mostly accepted the transition and was gracious. As more time passed, he was spending less time at work, and Jonathan was in full control. At that point, I asked Roger to take me to lunch. Toward the end of the meal, I got to the point. I asked him to take a pay cut given his new role; I felt it was necessary for the financial health of the company. And then, for the first time, I got the full Roger treatment I had heard so much about. He started with "Why, you little shit," and he only stopped when I retracted my request in full.

By 2004, Roger was only coming to his office a few days a week. When he came, he would spend his time on the antique chaise lounge in the corner, not at his desk. Finally, about two weeks after his last visit to the office, he passed away. The burial was at his family plot in an enormous cemetery in Queens. As Roger's ashes were placed in a mausoleum, I stood in the obvious chill between his wife Dorothea and his longtime assistant, Peggy. I did not know which one was the true love of his life, and I'm not sure they knew either. I could hear Roger saying, "Good luck with that, kid."

3.

The Flatiron

THE FLATIRON IS ONE OF THE MOST PHOTOGRAPHED BUILDINGS in the world, and rightly so. It is remarkably elegant. Approached from the north, the asymmetric triangle fools the eye and makes the building appear slimmer than it is. The windows in the point are curved, and they get narrower as they approach the top. The higher the floor, the sharper the point of the triangle becomes. There are lots of subtleties; fluted columns, arches, and large round windows, all enhanced by sculpted terra cotta. It is a seemingly delicate triangle among a sea of heavy squares and rectangles, the exclamation at the south end of Madison Square Park.

On my first morning, and every morning thereafter, I marveled at the building as I approached it. And for over twenty years, every day when I walked into my office, I was enchanted; the irregular shape, the high ceilings, the enormous arched windows, and the two columns in the point framing the Empire State Building.

The problem was everything else. The tiny elevators were the last water-powered hydraulic elevators in New York. They were original to the building, one hundred-plus years old. They broke down all the time, and only one company could fix them. They were slow, and they had to level at every floor before the doors would open, a sickening sort of bounce. Many of the windows were single pane, made from the original copper-coated wood that didn't seal. The water pressure was terrible, and there was no hot water; it got lukewarm at its best. The heating was steam, through ancient radiators with porous valves. The huge boiler was so old it had to be shut off in the middle of the day to rest, not a good thing in January. The wiring was ancient; space heaters would blow out the circuits. The bathrooms were minuscule; there was only one per floor, generally with a single stall. If you were a woman working on a men's room floor, you had to hit the stairs. And you would likely pass men in the same predicament coming the other direction. Waiting for an elevator was not an option.

The office space in the building was designed for small businesses. Each floor had two or three small suites of offices behind locked doors. Some of the small businesses kept their doors open, most notably the guy who made fezzes, the little red hats lining the shelves behind his desk. And there was a typewriter repairman, with his racks of old manual machines, his collector's sideline. There was no signage to tell you what was where on which floor. It was generally best to just step out of the elevator and wander for a bit.

When I started at St. Martin's Press, it was all very charming. For about a week. The elevators were so slow I took to walking up and down the eighteen flights. Winter mornings, in the pre-dawn dark, the wind blew papers off my desk through the closed windows. Typing with gloves on is no easy thing. It was cold in the winter, hot in the summer, and the elevators scared people. But nothing got to folks like the bathrooms. Everyone found something they didn't like about the bathrooms.

St. Martin's Press had started out renting a half floor in 1959, and by 1996, SMP was the largest tenant. We occupied 40 percent of the building. During my first speech to the staff after my arrival, I made a rash promise. Trying to infuse a new sense of promise and progress, trying to indicate that our company would prosper, and trying to signal that our living conditions would improve, I promised that I would get the elevators fixed. From that day forward we fought on two fronts: first to build a great publishing company, and second to make the Flatiron livable.

St. Martin's Press had a history of publishing hundreds of small books, each one at a small profit. Immediately we set out to buy bigger books and develop bestselling authors, while keeping the current model in place. It was lots of elbow grease, but it worked. The next step, and my next job a few years later, was to take all the publishing companies we owned in America and make them into a group. We called it Holtzbrinck Publishers. But no one could spell Holtzbrinck, and it certainly doesn't roll off the tongue. So, a few years later, we bought back our venerable publishing name, Macmillan, and used it for the US entity. We split off Tor from St. Martins, we brought in Farrar Straus and Henry Holt (both of which Holtzbrinck had previously purchased), and we made Picador a group-wide paperback line. We built a warehouse, we formed a group-wide sales organization, and we started an audiobooks division. We created four new children's publishing companies and formed a children's book group. We created new adult publishers and new imprints. We invested in production, IT, and infrastructure. For more than twenty years we grew faster than the industry every year but three. We published great books. By 2012, we became one of the "Big Five" publishers. On the higher education side of the business, based outside of the Flatiron, we did the same sorts of things, with the same sorts of results.

That was the easy part.

In the Flatiron Building, the elevators could not be fixed. Our lawyer tried to convince me to sue the landlord, but instead I kept butting my head against the wall. Finally, after a meeting with the landlord where I surprised myself by raising my voice and pounding my fist on the table, I relented. For the first time in my life, I agreed to sue someone. We hired a tough guy lawyer from Brooklyn. During the discovery process he made the legitimate request to see the elevator inspection records, starting in 1902. They arrived several weeks later by truck, countless cardboard boxes on pallets. The landlord called to settle the case the next week. We would get new elevators.

Next came the windows. There was some favorable language in our contract, and we finally got the landlord to agree to a deal. We got new windows, except for in the point, where we kept the curved, hand-crafted copper. In 2004, we negotiated a new lease. The company had grown enormously, and we had an option clause to take over the whole building. We did that. With some cash from the landlord, and some of our own, we remodeled.

I had always felt that in publishing, money should go to authors and selling their books, not to polished-up office space. That's a good thing because it's fair to say the remodel was non transformative. There was a new electric system and new broadband, but the heat still came slowly through banging radiators and the water never did get hot. The bathrooms were redone, to no discernable effect. After lunch you still had to occasionally walk eight flights to find a vacant stall, and that stall was still tiny. And there were still dozens of little office suites. If you walked the building, you would still go through over forty locked doors on twenty floors to see 820 people.

Work in the Flatiron had a unique rhythm; it was an odd ecosystem driven by the building. There was no cafeteria or common space, so the single stairwell served as the social hub. You would be walking downstairs from a meeting and run into someone waiting at the bathroom, and someone else would stop on their way up. "Hey, how was your weekend?"

The locked doors and rabbit warren offices made it hard to just drop by to see someone, and this made each floor and office suite feel like its own world. We kept the individual publishing companies as separate entities, and they all controlled the look and feel of the floors they occupied. There was no corporate branding and no similar design scheme. It was all about the individual publishers, and the books they published. And the physical space amplified this, both at the Flatiron Building and at our other offices.

But some things we did together. In 2010 we launched a company-wide sustainability effort, and we hired Bill Barry to run it. Bill and I decided the company should focus entirely on carbon emissions, and we would tackle scope one, two, and three emissions, something unheard of at the time.[4] After Bill's two-year massive effort to define our carbon footprint, we chose a somewhat arbitrary target: we would reduce our carbon emissions by 65 percent within ten years. The Flatiron posed interesting challenges with its window air conditioners and lack of infrastructure. And the companies were accustomed to their independence; they struggled with any corporate mandates. But the strong believers pushed hard, and our cause was worth every bit of the work. Everyone chipped in at the Flatiron and in every other building at the company. Macmillan just missed the reduction target at the end of a decade, but with an offset program, we were carbon neutral in seven years. The largest single complaint we got early in the program was predictable: the texture of the carbon-efficient toilet paper.

In the Flatiron, it was always about the bathrooms.

When our lease was up in 2018, we were very transparent in the decision process about what would happen next. Campaigns were

---

4   Scope 1 and 2 are those emissions that are controlled by the company, whereas scope 3 emissions are the consequence of the activities of the company but occur from sources not owned or controlled by it. In publishing, scope 3 includes paper and printing.

launched in the spirit of Brexit. Posters were made and put up all over the building, FLEXIT and REMAIN. The company was split on what they wanted the result to be, but the passion about the building was fierce. In the end, we had little choice but to move. We had outgrown the space, the construction logistics were daunting, and the new rent would be too high. We announced that we would indeed FLEXIT.

Over the years I always encouraged people to bring authors, agents, and accounts to my office. Pay me a visit and stand on the balcony to take in the view. They could just come in, no permission required. That little outdoor space between the columns, high up in the point, was magical, and I figured it should be shared by all. We had two employees who got married there, and two couples got engaged.

I reinforced my open-door message in the months before we moved; a last chance for one and all to stop by and see the office, bring whomever you like. For weeks it was a constant stream of employees with their friends from work, and with people they knew in the industry. They flew in from remote offices. They came with their students. They came with their kids and spouses. They came with their moms and with their dads.

We moved the company downtown to a neighborhood with much cheaper rent. We made the transition in the spring of 2019, a few floors at a time, week by week. I stayed in the Flatiron until the end. During the last week I wandered the almost empty building, remembering what happened over the years in all the rooms, and the people who sat in them. On the last night I stood alone in my empty office, looking at the Empire State Building, lit up blue and white. Sure, the Flatiron was inefficient and annoying, but the building had a soul of some sort, and we built something special there.

4.

The World of Letters

I N THE FLATIRON, AND IN THE BACK ROOMS OF PUBLISHING
houses everywhere, there are editorial files full of clutter and, on
rare occasion, from days gone by, written conversations between
skilled scribes, on paper, delivered by the US Postal Service. They
can be discovered by the curious.

My great-grandfather, the publisher nicknamed Effendi, received
such a letter from someone who had come to visit him in England,
in 1928. The visitor chose to address Effendi with the more formal
usage, Effendim. The letter opens with:

Effendim:

I have done ten solid days of duty in camp, and am again
free to go out: only instead of that I write you a line to recall
the very golden day we had. Do you know, it was all exqui-
site? Kingswood, Kipling, Knole, Ashdown Forest, the lunch.
Years since I drove, lordly, in a pleasure car: the R.A.F. has its
transports, of course, but that is hardly driving.

It rambles on for a bit, and then there is this, from a paragraph in the middle: "I have a design of sliding down some odd day if he permits it, and I achieve it, with Bernard Shaw & Mrs. Shaw. She is quaint & comfortable, and fresh, & kind. G.B.S. is exciting, per contra. Together they are like bacon and eggs, a harmony in blue and silver. I fear I talk nonsense."

The letter ends with: "Yours ever, T. E. Shaw" followed by "I've had twinges of conscience, since, that perhaps I tempted you to overdo things that day. I am so indecently fit and durable. I hope you are not ill or tired, even."

Shaw is a name the writer of the letter chose from a telephone book (Shaw being the first name he encountered that contained four letters which was also the top entry on a left-hand page). He was probably still in his late thirties when he wrote the letter, a young man who was trying to escape his name and famous past. In that famous past he was known as T. E. Lawrence, or more commonly, Lawrence of Arabia.

Two years after I started at Doubleday, I found a remarkable file that contained a four-letter exchange between Sam Vaughan, Doubleday's renowned editor-in-chief, and his author, William F. Buckley. The letters were verbal jousting between a left-leaning editor and the loudest conservative voice of his time. It was all smart, and there was clear fondness between them. There was a running theme concerning the Roman vomitorium, pages of it back and forth: historical references, modern parallels, vivid descriptions of a vomitorium in use, and speculation as to who might use one if it were available today. Lofty intellect on display, with roots firmly planted in potty humor.

* * *

Later, when I was at Simon & Schuster, I found a letter dated October 3, 1938. It was addressed to Max Schuster, and it described

102

a movie that was being made, based on a Simon & Schuster book. "All of us here feel we have a real hit and are quite happy over the way it is shaping up, although it is going to be another two years before it is ready for release." The letter was signed "Walt." In fact, it would be three years before Disney released *Bambi*.

Recently, I stumbled on a thank you note, this one written in 1985 from an author named Winston Groom to his publisher at Doubleday, Frank Cermak. Frank had taken Winston to a Mets game, and the note came in the voice of the main character in Winston's recent novel. It started with this line: "My Mama tole me to rite an thank you an all them good fellers an ladies that peddles books for your stow for takin me to the base-ball game." The note went on like that for a full page. It was signed Forrest Gump.

* * *

I found, and received, a lot of letters at work. Many were remarkable for their writing; many were remarkable for their content. A small number were remarkable for both. And then there was the letter I got in 1996 from Pat Conroy. I remember where I was sitting when I read it, and I remember exactly when the hair on the back of my neck stood up.

I was about to start my job at St. Martin's Press when the Emma Tennant story blew up. SMP had purchased the rights to publish a second sequel to *Gone with the Wind* from the Margaret Mitchell estate and had commissioned Emma to write the book. Emma had done her best, but SMP and the estate had decided it wasn't good enough and had rejected it. There was a noisy squabble. The first sequel, *Scarlett*, had been an embarrassment (Janet Maslin of the *New York Times* had called it a "stunningly uneventful 823-page holding action"). The estate could not afford another stumble.

It is hard to overstate the popularity and cultural importance of *Gone with the Wind*. The book was published in 1936. It was the #1 fiction title that year, and the next. It won a Pulitzer Prize in 1937. There have been thirty million copies printed, and in 2014, seventy-eight years after publication, a Harris poll determined it was the second favorite book of American readers, right behind the Bible.

The 1939 movie won ten Academy Awards, including best picture. When adjusted for inflation, it is the highest grossing movie of all time. In the four years after its release, sixty million tickets were sold in the United States, close to half the population of the country. In total, the movie has sold over 200 million tickets in North America.

In the middle of all the ruffled feathers of the Emma Tennant problem, Pat Conroy wrote a letter to the agent for the Mitchell estate, with instructions to forward it to Sally Richardson and me. Pat was a bestselling author at Doubleday and one of the leading figures in late twentieth-century Southern literature. His acclaimed novel *The Prince of Tides* had been made into a 1991 movie that was nominated for an Academy Award for Best Picture. He was an extraordinary novelist, and he proposed to walk in Margaret Mitchell's shoes.

The letter was handwritten on lined paper. The agent, Owen Laster of William Morris, sent it to Sally Richardson, the president of SMP, with a typed transcription. Sally sent both to me. The typed version was three pages long, single spaced. Pat wrote:

> I feel I am entering a cathedral my mother would want me to stay out of. My main concern is that I would write a book that would be a parody or a caricature of GWTW. Margaret Mitchell struck such a rich motherlode with her narrative that those of us who follow her will seem timorous and mice-like in comparison. Knowing this and understanding in my

bones that my task is impossible, let me tell you what I have in mind.

And further on he continued:

I will try to write for you and The Estate a better book than GONE WITH THE WIND. I will fail and I know I'll fail as I write these words. But I want you to know the degree of passion and ambition and terror I bring to the table . . . I would like to write a companion volume to GONE WITH THE WIND. I do not yet have a title, but let me make one up, Owen, on the spot, so you can see what I mean. A COLD EYE FOR THE HORSEMAN: The Memoirs of Captain Rhett Butler CSA. I would like to do the memoirs of Rhett Butler told in the first person, in his singular voice.

That is the moment the hair stood up on my neck.

He concluded the letter: "If I take this assignment and if this idea has any interest to you, then I will write this book as an act of great homage and joy. Because my mother read GONE WITH THE WIND as a girl, I write to you as a novelist today. This thrills me, Owen Laster, it simply sets me on fire."

When I finished the letter, I sat at my desk and contemplated the possibilities. This could be the biggest book of the year, or the decade, or maybe ever. I talked to Sally, and she agreed entirely. The problem was that Pat was contracted to Doubleday, SMP had licensed the rights from the Mitchell estate, and the estate had the right to approve what was written by the author.

And so the merry dance began. Doubleday and St. Martins had to find a way to publish the book together. Pat and the estate had to settle on terms, both financial and for approvals, and each had separate agents. Pat's editor at Doubleday was less than enthusiastic and worked against the project. But Jack Hoeft, the CEO of

Doubleday's parent company, wanted to get the deal done, and he and I worked to move things forward.

A few weeks before I started at SMP, I went into the wilderness on the northern coast of British Columbia. As my seaplane taxi approached the dock, the senior guide walked over, frowning. He opened the plane door. "I hope you are not one of those New York assholes. There is a guy named Jack holding for you on the sat phone." It was like that until I started at SMP, and for my first three months in the job.

But then, finally, we had a deal. Contracts were drawn up. The last issue was Pat's freedom to write what he wanted. Pat told the estate he planned to write Scarlett's death scene, with Rhett in the room. The estate said Scarlett could not die. And just like that, the book was stillborn.

Pat let us use his idea of telling Rhett's story, and Donald McCaig wrote a book that we published. But Pat Conroy's *A Cold Eye for the Horseman* remains one of the great books never written.

5.

Old Dogs, New Tricks

I WENT DANCING TWICE WITH LL COOL J (LADIES LOVE COOL James) and I can assure you that ladies do indeed love him. And so did everyone else as far as I could tell. When he came to our offices to pitch his book in 1996, rap was relatively new as a mainstream genre, and there was yet to be a big book by a rap star. I was a fan, but we all worried about the size of the market. He was amazing in our meeting, though, telling stories about his grandmother getting shot, about signing with Def Jam Records when he was sixteen, and generally putting forth huge waves of charisma. Thoroughly sold, we bought the book for what seemed like a huge sum.

He was a pleasure to work with, and he wrote a great book called *I Make My Own Rules*. But then we had to figure out how to sell it; the St. Martin's sales force at the time was not exactly in tune with rap culture. To address the problem, we asked LL to perform at a sales conference. He explained that to do that he would need to bring his equipment, and we would need insurance. It was going

107

to be costly. So we asked him to come and speak about his book instead, and he agreed.

When I arrived at St. Martin's, I was perplexed by the sorts of things people did to have fun at conferences. The preferred activity of the sales force was to watch movies in their rooms, or on a wild night to play Pictionary in the hospitality suite. I spent several conferences attempting to create a new normal. Beach games didn't work. Dancing didn't work. Karaoke night was a disaster. The plan for this meeting was to try a DJ, and I requested that he bring a selection of LL Cool J's songs.

The dinner that night was lively; LL made a great speech about his book. Oliver Stone was there for his new book, sitting at the next table. When dessert was served, I slipped out and walked down the hall toward the hotel lobby. On the left, I found the room where the dancing would be, and the DJ appeared to be ready. I asked him to watch me after the dancing started, and when I raised my right arm, to quickly put on "Momma Said Knock You Out."

Shortly after, some sales reps wandered into the room and the music started. The dance floor stayed empty. I started dancing with Barbara Andrews, our sales director at the time. For two long songs we danced alone, with the lights on bright and everyone watching. It was mortifying. Then the room started to get crowded, and out of the corner of my eye I saw LL standing in the doorway, glancing in. I waved my right arm at the DJ, and he put on the song.

LL hesitated a moment, but then he ambled through the door. Immediately, and I do mean immediately, a young woman asked him to dance. He obliged. Without him, Barbara and I would have been dancing alone out there forever, but now the dance floor quickly filled. As the first song finished, another young woman came forward and tapped out LL's dancing partner. No one tapped out Barbara. The DJ was on his game and put on another LL song. The place was hopping.

Next to the DJ there was a small wooden lectern with a tiny microphone, placed there in case I wanted to make a speech. About halfway through the third song, LL lifted his arms, palms out, head shaking. He walked up to the DJ and said, "Put that song back to the beginning." Then he slid behind the lectern, adjusted the mic, and cued the DJ. The sound quality was far from perfect, but did he ever belt it out.

Now the dance floor was packed. The song reached an instrumental point and LL shouted, "I want to see you jump." Some complied. He yelled again, "I want to see you jump!" The sales force was full of bookish folks; youth and athletic grace were not common traits. But on this night, in a mall hotel in New Jersey, they were giving it their best. Even those in gravity's tightest grip were briefly, gloriously, airborne. In my memory, the room is small, standard fare. In the back, on the left, Oliver Stone holds court amid the din. The dancers are beaming, with sweat on their brows, their arms over their heads, and their feet off the ground. "I want to see you jump."

6.

The Speaker

MY INSTRUCTIONS WERE TO MEET THE SPEAKER AT THE NEW York Public Library; this was going to be no dance party. We were scheduled to talk in a conference room for an hour. He was thinking of writing a book and was seeking guidance; I had been recruited to be his advisor. I did not agree with Newt Gingrich's politics, and I wasn't fond of his style, but he was a fascinating guy, and at the time he was at the peak of his power as Speaker of the US House of Representatives. I walked from our offices to the library on the appointed evening, up the front stairs past the two famous lions, and into the middle of a ceremony of some sort. The room was full of men in suits, marveling at the library's original copy of the Declaration of Independence, and at each other. I waited on the side as the Speaker held court.

There was a brief break in his conversation, and I stepped in to introduce myself. He gave me a smile and asked if I could possibly wait a few minutes. I was glad to. After a bit he made his way over, apologized for being late, and said he had a favor to ask. Could

I possibly ride across town with him? He needed to make some phone calls in the car, but then he would have an hour before his speech, and we could talk in the green room. No problem.

The car ended up being a black Suburban, complete with a security detail in a following car. I sat in the front with the driver, who was clearly Secret Service. The minute the doors closed we were wrapped in silence, the noises of the city muffled. Newt told me that everything I heard had to be confidential. I agreed. Then he picked up the phone and started dialing. It was a short ride across town and Newt never stopped. Dial talk. Dial talk. Dial talk. Dial talk. Dial talk. In fifteen minutes, I learned how government really works.

He was calling Republican members of the House and an occasional Democrat. They had passed a big bill that morning and Newt was calling to say thank you for their vote. Those were the nice calls. Then he would get on with a Republican member who had voted against the bill. That conversation was remarkably different. On every call he knew what future bills the member was interested in, and why. If they had voted yes on this day, he would tell them how he would support them on their bill of choice in the future. In the negative case, he would say things like "Bob, I cannot believe you let me down today. I know you want that third section in H.R. 263, and I'm not going to allow it on the floor. You need to think more before you vote in the future." Click. He had no notes, and he took no notes. The conversational tone shifted fluidly from harsh and angry to warm, and even playful, but his facial expression never changed. Call after call, he was a man at work, doing a job.

When the Suburban pulled to the curb, he clicked off. We got out, and he apologized for taking my time. In the green room we leaned on the furniture, him on the edge of a desk and me on a sofa arm. We spent an hour on what he should write, what he should look for in a publisher, how long things would take, and the various details of the publishing process. He was entirely focused, razor sharp, and funny. He went on to give his speech, and I took the subway home. A night out in New York, with a lesson from the Speaker.

My next lesson in politics would come from the other side of the aisle, in Washington, DC.

7.

Before Her Time

P AT SCHROEDER AND I WALKED INTO THE CONGRESSIONAL OFFICE building, a first for me, old hat for her. As we went through the metal detectors, the guard, a sullen-looking guy with graying hair, burst into a huge grin and nearly shouted, "Congresswoman!"

Pat lit up equally and responded with a hearty "Bobby!" They started to chatter. "How are the kids, did your boy go to college?"

This was not a singular event. As we walked the halls, I began to feel like an outsider at a high school reunion, a sorry sidekick to the prom queen. The first office we went into, a young woman looked up and her mouth fell open. She stammered, "Ya, ya, you are Pat Schroeder!" Pat gave her that big smile and said, "You're right! I am Pat Schroeder."

At that time, Pat was the CEO of the Association of American Publishers, and I was on the first of many lobbying trips to Washington as a board member of the AAP. Today we would be going to see lots of senior staff, with or without their respective members. I suspected Pat had brought me along for one reason. Senator Mike Enzi of Wyoming was running a committee that would be handling a bill we were concerned with. I had grown up in his state, and Pat probably thought I was the only senior executive in publishing who could talk like one of his constituents. As we arrived, the senator was rushing out for a vote. We said our quick hellos and goodbyes, then sat down with his chief of staff. Pat had coached me: "Never mind the details of the bill, just connect with the guy." And so, we started talking about the overcrowding in his hometown of Gillette, and by the end it was about fishing on Piney Creek (pronounced "crick" by both of us).

"Have you ever fished that stretch West of the county road bridge?"

"Yes, I got a big rainbow out of that pool by the big rock."

After about fifteen minutes, Pat weighed in with her request for the senator's help on the bill, and we left. We got the vote, and that started a series of treks to Enzi's office, always just Pat and me, even when other publishers were in town.

The next time I went to DC, Pat and I were riding on the underground tram in the Capitol building and she told me a funny story. I realized there were probably a lot more of those, so I asked her if she would, for the rest of the afternoon, tell me stories, whatever stories came to her mind as we traveled through the congressional buildings. Shortly thereafter, we passed a door to a senator's office. Pat said that it used to be Senator Alphonse D'Amato's office, and she described the weekly poker game he hosted there. Every week lobbyists would come to play, loaded with cash. The remarkable thing was that somehow the senator always won.

Next came the story of the congressional pool. When Pat was elected, she was told that only the men swam there, and some of them didn't wear suits. Pat's response was "Well, let's go see." Ignoring the pressure not to, she used that pool. The gentlemen put their suits on.

Then we passed the room where the Armed Services Committee meets. Pat was the first woman to serve on that committee, and the Republican chairman was not pleased. He told her he had no choice, he had to put her on the committee, but that didn't mean he had to give her a seat. From that day forward, Pat was forced to share a chair during the committee meetings with a fellow junior Democrat. One cheek on, one cheek off. The legend became that it was the only half-assed thing she ever did in Congress.

Later I got the story of how she won her first election. New to Colorado, her husband Jim got involved with local Democratic politics. When the seat in their district came open, it seemed certain that it would go to the Republican incumbent. The Democrats needed to run someone, and Pat agreed to be the sacrificial lamb. She ran her campaign out of her kitchen and got her message out through an army of students putting up fliers. On election night Jim and Pat sat in their living room to watch the returns come in. The numbers were a big surprise and the press started gathering in front of their house. The Schroeders, sure of failure, had made no victory plans, and Pat had no speech. A bit panicked, they bundled up their six-year-old and two-year-old, turned off the lights, snuck out the back, drove to the airport, and bought tickets to Disneyland.

* * *

I saw Pat Schroeder fully exercise her power just once, her hard edge on display. There was a bill regulating the level of lead in toys that was about to be passed into law. It was a good bill, but they made a mistake in committee negotiations and the definition of toys was expanded to include books. The bill was on a fast track. If it passed, it would require every children's book, past, present and future, to be tested for lead. And until tested, the books would have to come off the shelves, not only in stores but in libraries and classrooms.

117

Thinking it would be better to ask for forgiveness than permission, I skipped calling the other officers of the AAP board and dialed Pat directly. I asked her if she could find a way to stop the bill. Pat's always cheerful voice went away. She asked if I was telling her to stop it. I told her yes, I was telling her to stop it. She asked how important it was. I said it was very important that the bill be stopped. There was a moment of silence and then she said, "OK, I'll call you later."

Two days later Pat called. She said the bill would not go to the floor. I asked her what happened, and she said, "You told me I had to stop it, so I stopped it." I asked her how she managed that. She said she convinced the committee chair to keep it from reaching the floor until it was corrected. Completely unsatisfied, I asked her to give me all the details. After a sigh, Pat told me she had campaigned for the guy for years and that she had raised money for him in multiple elections. He owed her. So, she told him what she needed. He looked at her and said, "If I do this, are we square?" Pat said yes, and it was done. Years of favors and work, traded for one single action.

During much of Pat's time at the AAP she was involved in the struggle, in and out of court, between Google, book publishers, and authors over digital scanning. We had these massive three-way negotiating sessions, and early on Google offered to host them, in New York and California. Google was a young company then, and one of the first companies to offer a continuous supply of snacks, energy drinks, and food to all their employees. We all marveled at the vast array of delights, and on our first visit gladly accepted their offer of lunch. As we got ready to head to the cafeteria that day, Google's lead lawyer on the case approached Pat hesitantly. He hemmed and hawed a bit and finally came out with it. "Pat, we can't allow you to go to the cafeteria." Pat gave him a raised eyebrow. "You are too recognizable, and we don't want people wondering what you are doing here." Pat gave him a "You have got to be shitting me" look. There was some tension in the room. Never, in all the years of our Google battles, did their counsel look so hangdog. Pat, of course, was gracious. From that day forward, whenever we went to Google, she waited patiently in the conference room while we went to get our food, and the lawyer brought her lunch. A longtime fan of the congresswoman, he was abashed every time. I think it gave us negotiating leverage.

We were still fighting that case with Google when Pat's tenure as the CEO of AAP came to an end; she felt eleven years was enough. As Pat was leaving, she tried to convince me that I should have my portrait hanging on the wall with the past chairs of the AAP. Being the treasurer at the time, I disagreed with her. One day a framed picture arrived in my office with a note saying, "Here is what we will put up on the wall if you don't send us a portrait." It was a picture of me with Dolly Parton from an AAP event, and scrawled along the bottom in Pat's hand was an outrageous note.

Pat left us the way she left the House, full of energy and game to fight like hell for a good cause. Her goodbye letter was signed the same way all her notes and letters were signed. It was a thing that mystified publishers, we of the written word, a thing we could never quite grasp. She always drew a smiley face when she signed her name. She was using emojis before there were emojis.

8.

Monica and the Ever-Changing Tide

I N THE LATE NINETIES THE COUNTRY WAS PROSPEROUS, AND BILL Clinton was a generally admired president. He was plagued by a series of scandals, though, and a special prosecutor was named to investigate the Clintons' real estate dealings. That investigation led in turn to a series of allegations about sexual harassment, and eventually ended with charges against the president for perjury. The Republicans were righteously offended, while the Democrats and most of the press called it a witch hunt.

The perjury charge was based on Clinton's responses to questions about sexual relations with a twenty-four-year-old White House intern. When her name surfaced, Monica Lewinsky was taken away to a safe house by the FBI. The country was appalled and fascinated. Nobody knew who she was, or what she would say, but public opinion was brutally negative, and she was scorched in the press.

Monica decided to tell her story in a book, and she chose Andrew Morton to write it. Andrew was a charming guy and a good storyteller. [5] Armed with Andrew and heavy security, Monica came to New York to meet with publishers.

Sally Richardson, the president and publisher of St. Martin's Press, Bob Wallace, the editor in chief, and I went to meet Monica in a midtown conference room. She was full of energy, smart, and earthy. But what was astonishing was the fact that she was there in the first place. All of America was wondering who she was, and we were sitting across the table talking with her. She had some good stories about the president, and as she talked, I wondered if she had been in love with him, and more importantly, if she still was. It dawned on me that I could ask her. "Do you still love him?"

She paused, tears welled, and she replied, "I think so, yes." Oh my.

We took a cab back down to the office, full of excitement and plans. Monica had been clear that she needed the book to be a financial success; she would need money for what lay ahead. But it was more than that: she wanted people to know her side of the story. She had promised to do whatever she could to promote her book, and herself. We discussed a Barbara Walters special, the ratings champion of the day. Bob, before coming to work at SMP, had been a journalist and a producer for ABC News. I asked him if he thought Barbara would do the show, how he thought it would go, and what sort of lift it would give this particular book. His reply was succinct: "She will do it, the ratings will be huge, and if Barbara gets her to cry on air, we will sell tons of books."

---

5   Andrew Morton's last book, a biography of Princess Diana, had been an enormous success. Only after the book was published did it become clear that Diana had worked with him from the beginning, and the book was in some way a cry for help.

A few days later the agent ran an auction for the rights to publish the book. The heavy bidding was between just two publishers, which was a surprise. We lost. But the next day the agent called. Owing to internal pressures based on Monica's unpopularity, the winning publisher had backed out. Would we still be interested? Yes, we would.

When we announced that we would be publishing *Monica's Story* by Monica Lewinsky, the reaction was swift. The president of one of our publishing companies called me to say we should not publish the book. The head of our college textbook company called to say professors were angry, and we were losing course adoptions because of it. Agents called. Employees complained. My neighbors stopped me on the street to admonish me. The guy next door took me to task for several minutes after which he asked, "Have you actually met her?" Hearing that I had, he asked me what she was like, and what was she wearing. I nicely suggested to him that if he thought it was so wrong to publish her book, why was he so curious?

A few days later I flew to Germany for a board meeting. My boss, Dieter von Holtzbrinck, asked me in the politest manner if I would consider not publishing the book. I could see the distress on his face and the tension in his body. I apologized for the embarrassment I had obviously caused, but I was unequivocal that we would proceed. Dieter took measure of my response, nodded his head, and we went on to the next topic.

Sally and Bob were determined to go forward, and so was I. But the questions and complaints just kept coming. Going against public opinion is lonely when you hold the final decision, and I began to feel it. Looking for another point of view, I called Jonathan Galassi, the publisher of Farrar, Straus and Giroux, and asked him what he thought. His response was immediate. "She will be a historical figure, and her book should be published." We kept at it.

Monica and Andrew Morton wrote a good book, and St. Martin's did a good job publishing it. Barbara Walters wanted the first interview, and she cleared network airtime on the last night of January 1999, just hours before the book would go on sale. Halfway through the interview, Barbara asked a sentimental question, and Monica teared up briefly. Bob was right. The interview won Barbara the highest ratings of her career; with seventy million viewers, it was one of the most watched interviews of all time. The next morning there were lines in front of bookstores across the country. The morning news showed the lines and talked about the book that caused them. The phones were ringing off the hook. *Monica's Story* sold out across America that day and would go on to be one of the biggest books of the year.

Monica stayed in touch for a bit. She was constantly hounded by the press and tormented by an angry public. She led a strange life that year. The stories she told me about going on a few hard-to-get dates, and what would happen, were funny. They were also so very sad. She was proud of her book, and we were proud to have published it. Love her or hate her, she got to tell her story, and that is how it should be.

In hindsight, most people now see Monica in a different light. The cultural view of the events of those days, and her part in them, has shifted over time; it is hard to know how history will judge those who put themselves forward. Independent of lofty First Amendment debate, people, even those who are out of favor, have the right to have their voices heard. At times that makes publishing decisions extremely difficult, and on rare occasions it has made being a publisher a dangerous profession.

9.

All Grown Up

S EAN COMBS, BACK WHEN HE WAS PUFF DADDY, TAUGHT ME
that I was turning into the corporate guy I never imagined I
would be. Not that I ever met him. Sean was coming in for a meeting about doing a book, and he only had one time slot available.
I was supposed to be in a board meeting at the appointed time,
so I had a decision to make. I went to the board meeting. In that
moment I felt oddly grown up, and in truth, it made me melan-
choly. I got that feeling only once more, at a book convention in
Los Angeles.

I was working at Simon & Schuster when Viking Penguin published Salman Rushdie's *The Satanic Verses* in 1989. The world
was transfixed by the ensuing mayhem and so was I. Iran Supreme
Leader Ayatollah Khomeini placed a fatwa on Rushdie, which read,
"I am informing all brave Muslims of the world that the author of
Satanic Verses, a text written, edited and published against Islam,
the Prophet of Islam, and the Qur'an, along with all the editors
and publishers aware of its contents, are condemned to death. I

call on all valiant Muslims wherever they may be in the world to kill them without delay . . ."

Salman went into hiding with police protection for six years. There was a $6 million bounty on his head. The United Kingdom and Iran broke diplomatic relations. The book won the Whitbread Award as the outstanding novel of the year in the United Kingdom, but was publicly burned in Bradford, England. Two bookstores in the United States were bombed and the *Riverdale Press* newspaper office in New York was destroyed. The Norwegian publisher was shot and seriously injured. A translator was killed. About a third of American booksellers stopped selling the book, but most bravely carried on. I remember visiting the Viking Penguin offices at the time and seeing guard dogs in the lobby. The CEO, Peter Mayer, was regularly under armed guard.

It struck me as tremendously important and courageous. Freedom of speech in its pure form. People risking injury and death rather than stopping the publication of a book.

Ten years later, at Henry Holt, we would publish a Salman Rushdie novel, *The Ground Beneath Her Feet*. The fatwa was still officially in place, but there was no real perceived danger. He had published another novel after *The Satanic Verses* without incident. I had met Salman a few times and when we talked about the new book, he told me this would be his attempt at writing the great American rock 'n' roll novel. Fresh from his years behind locked doors, he seemed vital and eager. I marveled at the thought of him, and at the man himself.

The convention in Los Angeles was a typical book show. Lots of busy booths on a huge convention floor. Mobs of booksellers, publishers, and authors. I was standing in front of our booth when Salman came by, looking for me. We chatted for a bit and then he asked if I would care to join him that night for a party. He explained that he had a car and driver and that he was going to the Playboy mansion. Would I like to come?

The first two generations of Doubleday publishers: Effendi (with the flower on his lapel) and Big Nelson (the tall guy). Apparently, it was OK to wear shorts to work.

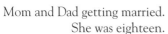

Mom and Dad getting married. She was eighteen.

The surprise pioneer wedding. Mom in pigtails with our dog Tom, and John Kings, now her second husband. Martha Gibbs is in the back holding her baby. I'm the kid in the cowboy boots, standing with my sister Ellen.

The one-room schoolhouse I attended for two years. It was built on a ranch in 1914. They moved it to the town of Ucross in 1916. After it closed as a school it became part of the Ucross Foundation. Annie Proulx was a resident there, and she wrote part of *Shipping News* in the building. Ucross has grown in recent years to a population of twenty-five.

Our family on Christmas morning, 1971. Freshman year of high school, braces, glasses, and playing cymbals in the Sheridan Broncs marching band.

Anthony Rubinstein, The Nose.

My father had an extraordinary social life. He had lots of tuxedos. Dad dated Jackie O when she worked at Viking, and then he hired her at Doubleday. The dating continued until whatever was going on suddenly stopped. I think they were friends, and he was helping her to distract the press. (Photo by Tony Palmieri/Getty Images.)

Connie and me with a Wild Thing. We were attending one of the first galas for Graham Windham, a child welfare and family support organization cofounded by Eliza Hamilton in 1806. I had just joined the board. I became the chair a few years later, and thirty-three years on I am still helping with the great work they do. That is my first and only tux.

A last-ditch effort in a Simon & Schuster bathroom. Ken Geist and I go with half beards to sell a book.

The Duchess of York in my Simon & Schuster office in Rockefeller Center.

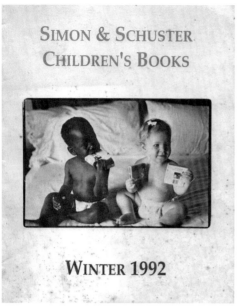

SIMON & SCHUSTER CHILDREN'S BOOKS

WINTER 1992

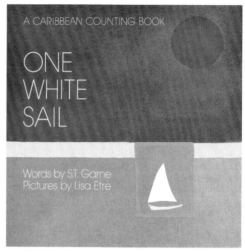

My first book, written under a pen name.

Publishing on an extremely tight budget. The seasonal catalogue featuring Ken Geist's son, Will, and my daughter Kyle having an early book club. (Photo credit to Connie.)

Rain or shine, I always went to work. In this case even when a blizzard closed the subways and the Brooklyn Bridge.

Dorling Kindersley was always fun. I'm the guy with the flower in my hair. The hippy with the wig and shades is Roger Priddy. We created a line of books together at DK, and he joined us later at Macmillan to start a successful global publisher called Priddy Books. We wrote a book together called *Fruitcake*.

My first trade show at St. Martin's Press with the extraordinary Sally Richardson. For twenty-six years she never ceased to amaze me.

LL Cool J pumps up the salesforce while Oliver Stone has a small confab on the other side of the room. John Murphy on the left, Oliver Stone in the middle, and Matthew Shear on the right.

Hanging out with Andrew Morton and Monica Lewinsky in the seventeenth-floor Flatiron conference room.

Pat Schroeder's suggested portrait of me for the wall at AAP.

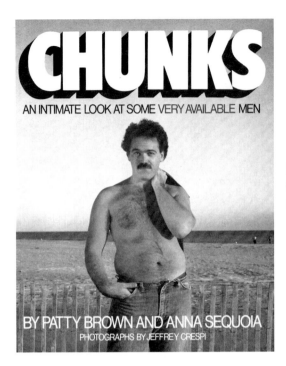

Matthew Shear on the cover of *Chunks*; he would do anything to sell a book.

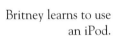

Britney learns to use an iPod.

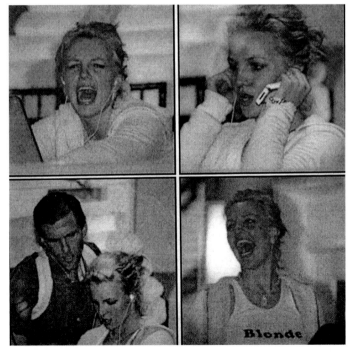

Surrounded by fantastic women in red dresses, Oprah and Pat Schroeder. The irrepressible Jane Friedman, CEO of Harper Collins, holding hands. On the far left is Richard Sarnoff, then co-chairman of Random House. He and I shared a foxhole for eight years as the lead negotiators for publishers in the Google Books settlement. Next to Richard is Bob Evanson of McGraw Hill. On the far right is Bob Miller, then president of Hyperion. In the years to come he joined Macmillan to start a new imprint called Flatiron Books. Flatiron's first title was *What I Know for Sure* by Oprah Winfrey.

Steve Kessel, the guy who was in charge of creating and managing Kindle for Amazon. I always enjoyed working with him, and others at Amazon, even when we locked horns.

The Flatiron. The view from the ground (with me standing on the ledge outside my office), the view from the sky (the tiny figures are my old friend Paul Shang and me), and the night view from my office. (Sky view photo by George Steinmetz. Ground view photo by John Madere.)

 **REMAIN!**

A poster from the Remain vs Flexit battle when we were deciding whether to stay or leave the Flatiron Building.

On their last day in the Flatiron, the folks at Tor spontaneously painted on all their walls.

The offices of FIRST SECOND are located in the magnificent FLATIRON building, in New York City...

To some it's like a proud ship sailing uptown through Madison Square...

... an impression confirmed by visiting the building's top floors and one of the finest offices in NYC: that of JOHN SARGENT, head of Holtzbrinck, USA.

I met Mark Siegel at a wedding. Shortly thereafter he joined us to start First Second, the highly successful graphic novel imprint. He drew this cartoon and posted it on the First Second/ Holtzbrinck website. The next day he asked me if it was OK. It pushed the edge of appropriate, but I loved it.

My successor Don Weisberg, Louise Penny, and me. We had just discovered that Louise made #1 on the *Times* bestseller list. Again. The three of us remain great friends.

An Elton John party in small-town Australia. The Aussies love to dress up. Charlotte Ree (marketing manager) in the front, Tracey Cheethan (publicity and marketing director) in the back.

For my twentieth anniversary at Macmillan, I took most of the US senior management and their families out to the ranch in Wyoming on my dime. I wanted to express a personal thank you. The rock this group is standing next to is the petrified trunk of a fifty-five-million-year-old tree. (Photo by Tenoch Esparza.)

Bobby Gibbs with one of his hand-rolled cigarettes. If you look into his left eye, you can see a smile hiding. Maybe. (Photo by Dudley Whitney.)

The ranch. There are fewer horses around these days, but the view never changes.

When the most important things began. Connie and me a year after we met. I still wear that belt, but the tail is shorter.

I had flown to Los Angeles that morning. I hadn't gotten much shut-eye that week, and I had meetings stacked up back-to-back for the next two days. And Salman, at this point, was well known to enjoy the late-night party scene. Imagining myself waiting until the small hours for a ride home, I gulped and said I could not go. He went off without me, and I spent some hours questioning myself. The front page of the papers the next day showed Salman with a Playboy Bunny on his right arm and another on his left. He reported the Jacuzzi had been great.

I got a good night's sleep.

The Satanic Verses was an extraordinary commercial success and was a defining moment in East/West culture. It sparked numerous international incidents. It helped shape a generation of publishers around the world on the importance of free speech, and the power of a novel. At the center of it all was the man who wrote the book and suffered the consequences of doing so, including an assassination attempt in 2022, thirty-three years after the book was published.

Like many, I was inspired by Salman and the publication of *Satanic Verses*. All that inspiration didn't help his rock and roll novel, though; it was not a commercial success. And I probably wouldn't have had much fun at the Playboy Mansion. But somewhere inside of me, my younger self still has regrets about taking a pass. I suspect Salman knew how to have a good time.

10.

Some Authors Like It Hot

S ALMAN RUSHDIE HAD ALWAYS BEEN CHARMING TO ME, EVEN when things were difficult. But being published is a tough and emotional process, and many authors strain to retain a cheerful demeanor. They are all passionate about their work, and rightfully so. This causes the occasional uncomfortable moment, and sometimes it gets intense. A few authors have tempers, and tempers flare.

The Coach

Bobby Knight, one of the greatest basketball coaches of all time, was not happy. We were publishing his book, and things were rocky. The day after the book went on sale, he was scheduled for a radio interview, and he missed it. The radio host spent the airtime thrashing him. It was not clear where the fault lay for the mistake; there was lots of finger pointing. Bobby was clear in his own mind that the mistake was ours, and he wanted to talk to me. He was steaming mad, but he was also leaving on the 6:00 a.m. train to

129

Washington the next morning. We arranged to meet on the platform at 5:45.

He walked up, and we shook hands. He was tense. No small talk: here it comes. His eyes were flashing; his face turned red. He was loud, his voice carried over the roaring of the trains and the bustle of the crowd. The words came out like weapons; they were personal and designed to hurt. At his first pause, I apologized. There was another short blast of venom and then it was over. There was some small talk; he was charismatic. He had a place in Wyoming, and we agreed to meet out there someday. Then he got on the train, and I went to work. As I walked across town, in my mind I saw the old film clips; Bobby throwing chairs at his players, the rants at referees. I had gotten just a small taste on that train platform, and I had no urge for a full meal.

A year later he called. He was headed out to Wyoming; would I be there? No, but I set him up to go fishing at the ranch. He showed up and caught some fish. The next weekend when I talked to my mom, she said how nice he was. She also told me it was good that I'd stayed in touch with my high school basketball coach.

The Actor

Alec Baldwin was surprised that I answered my own phone. It set him back for just a second, and then he wound up. We were scheduled to publish his book about divorce, and his former wife had just attempted to stop us. Alec had convinced himself that we were going to back down and pull his book. As he talked, I could feel his anger building. Then suddenly he was yelling into the phone. He was on a street corner, in public, but he was letting it all go. I tried to interrupt him, but he just blasted on. Finally, I raised my voice: "Alec!"

He stopped talking, and I explained that these things happen; it was nothing new for us. Yes, she was trying to stop the book from being published, but she was also trying to make us more careful about what the book said. Early notice that a book may be libelous makes the publisher more susceptible to a negative outcome in court. I promised we would publish the book as it was, and that he did not have to worry. It was like throwing a switch. There was no tension in his next sentence, all the anger gone. I thought how exhausting it must be for him.

The Lord

We had been publishing the notorious Jeffrey Archer for years. He had started a writing career in 1974, not out of passion, but to stave off bankruptcy. With the publication of his second novel, *Kane and Abel*, he became hugely successful, and in the years that followed he would sell over 320 million books. He was a member of Parliament at twenty-nine. He is a former deputy chairman of the Conservative Party. He went to jail for two years on a perjury charge. He is a Life Peer as Baron Archer of Weston-super-Mare. He produced a successful charity concert to raise money for the Kurds. He wrote three plays and starred in one. He is a Lord. And on this day, he was seriously pissed off.

Lord Archer's books top bestseller lists around the world, particularly in the United Kingdom and the former British territories. But not since 1979 had he been #1 on the *New York Times* bestseller list, and that bothered him. It was the summer of 2015, and his latest novel was set for publication in the fall. That July, Apple had given Macmillan an opportunity. Eager to boost ebook sales, Apple had constructed a promotion to aggressively sell a single title through all their devices around the world. Archer's new novel was our logical global choice, but in order to spread the wealth and maximize our sales, we had chosen to promote a different title in the US market. Jeffrey soon discovered that he wasn't going to be featured on Apple devices in the United States, the one market that mattered most to him. He asked who had made the decision, and discovered it was me. I was summoned to his apartment in London, posthaste. Geoff Duffield, who managed Jeffrey's marketing out of our London office, joined me.

Jeffrey lives in a modern apartment tower on the Thames River. There is normal security downstairs and a normal elevator. We got in and pushed the top button, the one that says P. The elevator door opened into his apartment and a hallway led to the right. That's where normal took a holiday. The hallway is lined with remarkable impressionist art. At the end of the hall, in a pool of light, hangs a Monet of the Houses of Parliament. The hall then turns to the left and opens into the living room, and a long wall of floor-to-ceiling glass. In the center of that panoramic wall, across the river, is Parliament itself. In front of this view, Geoff Duffield and I arrived for our audience with Lord Archer.

Jeffrey and his agent, Jonathan Lloyd, were sitting in stuffed chairs, Jeffrey on our left, Jonathan with his back to the view. Jonathan jumped up to greet us; Jeffrey remained seated. The Lord was all business. He held up his iPhone and snapped, "By any chance, Mr. Sargent, do you know what this is? There are hundreds of millions of these around the world. People use them a lot. Can you please tell me what it is?"

I replied, "That is an iPhone."

"Exactly," he said acting surprised that I would know. It went on from there, with his voice rising in volume. I glanced at Geoff. All the color had drained from his face, and there was a thin line of sweat on his brow.

Finally, Jonathan interrupted the tirade and asked Jeffrey, "Shouldn't we at least invite them to sit down?" We sat and Jeffrey started up again. He questioned my loyalty, my competence, my intelligence, and my leadership. He berated me in a steady stream with occasional breaks to ask belittling questions. His anger was less for show now—he was getting truly heated. I thought Geoff might pass out. At the end of the rant Jeffrey sat back, seemingly drained. Then he leaned forward, animated again. "I have been doing extensive research on you, Mr. Sargent, and I have been very thorough." A pause. "You, sir, are a lion." And then, with real emotion, "Why won't you be a lion for me?"

I assured him I had indeed been working on his behalf. I told him his current book would not be number one on the list, that there were just too many other big books coming out the same week. I then promised him we would get him to number one with his next book. Making it up as I went, I explained that we would put a senior executive in charge of the publication, and that we would invest all the necessary resources. I told Jeffrey he needed to write a great book; it would have to be a step up. Jeffrey committed to do that, and then seemed satisfied that the problem was solved. The meeting became conversational. We stood by the windows, and he pointed out the various landmarks. As I turned to leave, he said, straight-faced, "I hope the next time you come I won't have to throw you out the window." I responded that if it came to that, I would rather he throw me out the front window, so I might have a shot at landing in the river.

A week later I got a report back from Geoff. Jeffrey had informed him after the meeting that "You have to respect a man who can take a battering like that" and "I like the fact that he has no concerns regarding his personal appearance, and absolutely no interest in clothes whatsoever."

Thankfully we found someone with great skill and energy who was willing to manage the single title. Jeffrey wrote a great book, and we published it well. It hit #1 on the *NYT* list, and Jeffrey wrote me an extremely nice thank you note. We corresponded occasionally after that, and I always enjoyed hearing from him. He was a pleasure to publish. Years later, he called me, irate at our owner who had done a bad deed in his eyes, and full of kind words for me. He insisted repeatedly that I join him for lunch in the House of Lords, which I plan to do, maybe even in a jacket and tie.

11.

A Good Reason to Be Late

H E WALKED INTO THE ROOM ALONE. HE WAS TALLER THAN I thought he would be, and thinner. I shook his remarkable hand. It was thick and beefy, the skin on the back a pale white. The palm felt like a truck driver's, but the fingers were long and tapered; they were graceful, almost elegant.

I had come to this chain hotel in Stamford, Connecticut, to offer publishing advice as a favor for a friend. I was on my way to a meeting in Boston, and the hotel would be a brief stop in my day. I had arranged for SMP's marketing guy, John Cunningham, to join me. My train was on time, and I walked to the hotel. Feeling foolish, I told the man at the desk I was here to see a guest, and I used the fake name I had been given.

A very large person came out of the back. He was in a suit, all business, with the curly wire in his ear that says security. He told me his name, and as we walked to the elevator I asked if that was his real name. He replied, "Of course not." We walked in silence down a long hall that led to a hospitality suite. In the suite, the shades were drawn, and it smelled of stale cigarette smoke. There were two chairs and a couch floating in a large space in front of a fake fireplace. Security motioned to a chair and said, "He will be here shortly," then he left to stand at attention outside the door. I sat in the dim light alone.

And then, there he was, at the height of his fame, with his remarkable hand. He wore aviator dark glasses that were impenetrable; they had a flat black surface, and he never took them off. His jacket had a military feel; his hair was long and stringy. And yes, his nose was strange. Hello Michael Jackson.

Michael took the other chair, and a few minutes later John showed up and settled on the couch. Michael had a series of questions, which John and I answered to the best of our ability. I had been at Doubleday when we signed his first book, and I knew its troubled history. Jackie Onassis had worked hard as the editor, but the whole project had been a gloss over and the sales had been a disaster. I talked to Michael about why this had to be different. He would have to show himself to the reader this time. For the book to work he had to share his thoughts and, more importantly, his emotions.

He didn't seem to like that much. He asked a lot of questions about a recent book by Madonna. It was titled *SEX* and had a metal die-cut cover with wire spiral binding. He had questions about the physical object, and about the content. He seemed a bit agitated. Finally, he blurted out, "She showed her patootie! Will I have to do that?"

I kept a straight face. I did not look at John. "No, Michael, let me assure you that no one wants to see your privates."

The conversation was full of energy; there was banter back and forth. As things wound down, I asked him about his remarkable flexibility. He told a few stories, and then John, now fully splayed on the couch, said he was highly flexible as well. John is a large man—think John Candy or John Goodman large—and a publishing guy. Then he made a simple statement: "I can put my foot behind my head."

I could not conceive that it was possible. Michael and I stood up from our seats. No way! I turned to Michael and said, "I would really, really like to see that. How about you?"

Michael started giggling, he clapped his hands, and then in a high-pitched gush he said, "Yes, please. Oh yes, yes." John looked at us standing there, then he scootched forward on the couch, grabbed his left foot, pulled it over his head, and placed it behind his neck. Michael burst into applause, by all appearances much more excited than he was two nights later when he received his Grammy.

John went home and I got on the train. But it was a later train than I had planned, and I arrived late in Boston for my meeting with Joan Feinberg. Joan ran our Boston office, she was a great publisher, and her schedule was always tight. But when I explained why I was late, she didn't seem to mind. Pop stars will do that for you.

12.

The Mystery Man

STARTING WHEN MY DAUGHTER WAS NINE AND MY SON WAS four, we usually spent Christmas week skiing at Windham Mountain in New York. To keep things interesting while they learned, I put the skis away and tried my hand with a snowboard. It was fun for the kids to watch Dad giving it his all in the terrain park, but the hard ice of the Catskill Mountains took a regular toll. Every year I left the ski hill and went directly to our college sales meeting, and for four years in a row I arrived with some sort of injury. This year I had torn my collarbone off my right shoulder.

Does that hurt? Yes, it does. Unfortunately, it also requires a butterfly brace, a medieval sort of contraption. The brace requires someone to pull, quite hard, on a series of straps that force the collarbone to bend downward toward the shoulder. It needs to bend downward because otherwise it sticks out beside your neck. I discovered that having someone bend your collarbone by brute force is an unpleasant process, and on the doctor's advice I did it only once a day. At this conference I would get up early and struggle into a button-down shirt, wander down to breakfast, grab some poor soul who was just trying to drink their coffee, and ask them to administer the torture. It was not a good way to start their day, made worse no doubt because I was not my hygienic best: I had no ability to raise my right arm, so there had been no hair combing, no hair washing, no shaving, and no effective teeth brushing for several days.

On the first day of conference there was an afternoon break, with time enough to hit the gym. I figured not having a functional right arm was no reason to miss working out. Still in my brace, I decided it was probably best to just tuck my dress shirt into my gym shorts. This was not a good look. When I arrived at the gym, there was a large man standing in front of the door. He informed me that the gym was closed, there was one woman finishing up in there, and then they were going to be blowing out the air conditioning ducts. Undaunted, I said, "I'm from New York, dusty air doesn't bother me. I only have one break today, and I need to get some exercise." He thought to argue, but I think my appearance had some effect. He looked up and down the hall, then opened the door and let me in. I didn't consider that he might be security.

It was a nice gym on the ground floor. The exercise machines looked out through tall windows to a lush lawn and a quiet street. There was a young blond woman jogging on a treadmill in gray sweats. I plugged my iPod into the wall to charge it, then hopped on a stationary bike and started to pedal. We were alone together in the large space, working out side by side, looking out the window in silence.

A car pulled to a stop on the road outside. A guy with a camera got out, pointed it at the side of the building, and started taking pictures. A few minutes later another car pulled up, another guy got out, and he too started taking pictures. Both cameras had huge lenses, both seeming to be pointed straight at us. I looked over at the young woman; she seemed oblivious. But she looked friendly enough, so I cleared my throat, pointed at the photographers, and asked, "Does this happen to you often?"

She said "Yes." We went back to silence.

After a few turns of the pedals, I said, "I should probably know who you are, but I don't."

She replied, "I am a singer." I pedaled some more, she kept jogging.

I said, "You are going to have to help me more than that."

She said, "My name is Britney."

I was working out with Britney Spears. As we pedaled and jogged, more cars arrived. The road filled with photographers snapping away. Britney got off the treadmill and got on the bike next to mine. She asked how long I ride for; I told her today for about an hour, but sometimes for two or three. She said she liked to change machines frequently, then asked how I keep from getting bored while staying on a bike for so long. I answered that I usually listen to music and pointed to my iPod on the floor. She asked, "Is that one of those iPod things?" Britney Spears had just called an iPod an iPod thing.

I asked, "Do you mean to tell me you have never used an iPod?" She gave me a look, so I asked her if she would like to try mine.

She was instantly gung ho. I climbed off my bike, trying not to think about my bad breath, three-day stubble, weird brace, and sweaty dress shirt. I got my iPod and asked her what type of music she liked. I suggested that I had plenty of country. She laughed and asked if I might possibly have some pop.

I remembered that I had one of her songs, a cover of Bobby Brown's "My Prerogative." She struggled with the large earbuds, so I assisted. Then I cranked up the song, handed her the iPod, and got back on my bike. She started to murmur along softly while she pedaled. Then, glancing over and seeing my grin, she started singing full bore. The whole song, beginning to end. And now there were lots of cameras, all snapping away.

The song ended and she asked for more, so I showed her how to choose more songs. After a bit, the gym door opened and in came Kevin Federline, her boyfriend at the time. She asked if I had any Aerosmith, which I did. I put some on and she made him listen. He just seemed glum, and she got after him for not being more excited. He left. Britney and I were still pedaling. Her phone rang, and she talked to someone about how the other girls have tiny little dogs, so shouldn't she have one too? We pedaled some more and then she got off the bike, we chatted for a minute, and she said she had to get to work. She proceeded to roll up her sweatshirt and roll down her sweatpants. Work apparently was practicing her latest dance routine with a bare midriff. All that time I had been wondering what the big deal was about Brittany Spears. Watching her dance in the mirror in front of the bike, I understood. The cameramen outside were in full red-carpet mode.

I went back to my room and called home. I got everyone on the line and reported on my bike ride to nowhere with Britney Spears. Then it was back into pants, no change of shirt, and down to dinner. After the meal, I chucked my prepared speech and told the gathered Macmillan employees about my afternoon instead. No corporate strategy, just a tale of a pop star and a guy whose kids thought he was cool, at least for a day. Everyone seemed to appreciate the story, but no one rushed to stand next to me afterward.

I flew back to New York the next day on the red-eye. I was heading to my office early in the morning, and I got on the elevator with a guy from the IT department. He asked me, "How is Britney?" Laughing at my shocked expression, he said, "You are all over the fan sites."

And indeed, I was. As bad as I looked, for an instant I flirted with fame as Britney's "Mystery Man." Or, on other more accurate sites, as "some guy teaching Britney how to use an iPod."

13.

Fortunate Son

I T STARTED SIMPLY ENOUGH: GEORGE W. BUSH WON THE Republican nomination for the presidency. Tom Dunne, a publisher at St. Martin's Press, decided to commission a quick biography. It would have some light research, but mostly it would be a cut and paste job from the public record. He hired James Hatfield to write the book on a very short deadline, all standard operating procedure. The title of the book reflected the candidate's inherent familial advantages: *Fortunate Son*.

Jim went to work. He found some confidential sources and uncovered some stories. He submitted a draft, and we gave it an in-depth legal review. Jim kept good notes. Many of the details in the book had been published before, and when we checked the sourcing it all came back clean.

Rumors about the book began swirling in Republican political circles and we got a few calls challenging the veracity of some of the reporting. In particular, there were concerns about a story in the book that the nominee's father, President George H. W. Bush, had disapproved of his son's girlfriend because of her Hispanic heritage. We dug into the sourcing on that story and discovered it had indeed been published elsewhere.

The next week my phone rang, and the caller identified herself as President Bush's attorney; she was calling on his behalf. We exchanged brief pleasantries, she explained why she thought our book had errors, and then she got to the point: "The president has authorized me to use whatever means necessary to stop the publication of this book." I told her in no uncertain terms that we would be publishing the book. It was a short phone call. After I hung up, I pondered the term "whatever means necessary" and what that might mean coming from a guy who used to run the CIA.

I called Benita Somerfield, an old pal who ran the Barbara Bush Foundation and had friends in high places. She agreed that "whatever means necessary" was not ideal wording and that she would try to help. Benita brokered a deal. We would show the president the language he had concerns about, and we would add his denial to the final manuscript. The book went to press with the added language, and I thought our problems were behind us. Boy was I wrong.

We gave the *New York Times* an early copy of the manuscript, and they sent a reporter to Texas to do research. They were excited about the book. Of particular interest was the confirmation of a long-standing rumor that the nominee had been busted for cocaine in his youth, and that his dad had helped solve the problem. The publishing date neared, and we shipped books to stores across the country. We held back on TV publicity to give the *Times* the chance to break the story. It all felt right; there was news in the book.

Then, just days before we published, the *New York Times* went silent. The reporter would only say they were nervous about getting corroboration. Rumors started surfacing that there was a problem with the author. The unraveling had begun.

A Republican operative leaked a story that James Hatfield had a criminal record. The phones rang with press calls. That afternoon, reporters from 60 *Minutes* showed up in the lobby of our building with cameras, asking bewildered employees for comment. Demands to cancel the book started to pour in. It was the lead story in the news. The pressure built, hour by hour.

The next day we had a meeting in my office. There were ten of us, the department heads and the people directly involved with the book. We discussed our options, none of them easy. We decided at the end of the meeting to keep moving forward with the publication. Three hours later there was a report by Rush Limbaugh that the CEO of St. Martin's had called a meeting of the top brass to discuss the future of the book.[6] He placed the meeting in the Flatiron, he had the content about right, but was off by one concerning the number of people in my office.

That night, unknown to us, President Bush booked himself onto a TV news show for an interview about the book. On air he said it was full of lies. He said he had told the CEO of the publishing company that it was full of lies and that he had been ignored. He said this guy was a bad character. I was mortified and could not bring myself to watch the tape. Benita told me that according to the inner circle, the last time the president had been this angry at someone it had been Saddam Hussein. That did not make me feel better.

Jim Hatfield was in town the next day to do publicity, and we insisted he come to the office. He spent a few hours going over his sourcing with our lawyers. He said that many rumors had come up over the years on the cocaine story, some of which were printed. Then he claimed to have confirmed the story with a confidential

---

6   I recall that it was Rush Limbaugh who first reported the story. There is a chance that it was Matt Drudge, and that Rush followed. In fact checking, no one was certain, so I stayed with my recollection.

source, a high-ranking Republican from the Bush campaign, Jim's version of Deep Throat. The source had been clear on the details and the role played by the president, back when his son, now the candidate, was young. Our lawyers would have preferred two sources, but given Jim's overall reporting, they thought we were on firm ground.

There was considerable tension when Jim came to my office after meeting with the lawyers. Agents and authors had been calling steadily, some to argue that we should keep selling the book, and some to say we should pull it. Bookstores wanted a statement from us, and now. The press was unrelenting.

We had a decision to make. Jim and I sat in chairs at a slight angle to each other, he to my right, me to his left. There were a few other St. Martin's people sitting across from us. We talked briefly about the informant. He told us it was a very highly placed official in the campaign who had provided the details. He told us that the source had demanded they meet at a lake in Texas. When Jim arrived, the source asked him to sit in a small boat, which he then rowed onto the lake. Directional microphones were a concern. Once safely away from shore the source gave a convincing account of what had happened. Jim leaned forward as he told the details of the story, his face tense, his words coming fast. There were no hesitations, no shifting in his seat. Our publisher and our lawyer had tried to get him to reveal his source, and now it was my turn. I explained how difficult our situation was, and Jim responded that he would never reveal the name.

The question about his source was the warmup. The central reason we had called the meeting was to discover if the allegations about his own criminal record were true. I explained to Jim that it was critically important that he answer my questions truthfully. I moved my chair to face him more directly. "Jim, have you ever been convicted on a felony charge?"

He was clearly insulted. "Of course not." I asked if he had ever been indicted in a felony case. "No." I asked about misdemeanor indictments and then misdemeanor convictions. He became emotional. "No, no, no." And then he jutted his chin, his face reddened, and his voice rose. "John, why can't you see it? This is exactly how the Republicans operate and you know it. This is typical political dirty tricks; they are trying to discredit me. I can't believe you would fall for this."

I brushed his protest aside and told him he had better give me the truth and give it to me now. "Do you have a criminal record of any kind in Texas or any other state in the union?"

He replied, "Jesus, John, I've had a couple of speeding tickets and that's it, period." As he got up to leave, he asked me if we would continue to support the book. I said we would.

Alone now in my office, I pondered his responses. The Republican strategist Lee Atwater had indeed done this sort of thing in earlier campaigns. And the current operative in the role, Karl Rove, was no stranger to political dirty tricks. He was a guy deeply versed in the ends justifying the means. What we needed was more information.

I had read a lot of thrillers; it comes with the job. If our current situation were fiction, this would have been the moment to employ a private detective. So I called John Murphy, who was handling our publicity, and asked him to call Pinkerton in Dallas. I told him to ask if they could find any criminal record of any kind for James Hatfield. I also suggested speed would be important; time should be measured in hours, not days.

By the next afternoon the drumbeat out of Texas was getting louder. The *New York Times* pulled their story and all the coverage of the book they had planned. They told us they had found nothing that proved Jim wrong on the cocaine allegation, but they also had found nothing to prove him right. We were in limbo. The book was now on sale and it was doing well, lots of interest driven by the intense media coverage.

Because of the leak to Limbaugh, it was now a very small group involved in our decisions at Macmillan. We met regularly to digest news, weigh options, and decide on operational matters like printing more books. In a rare quiet moment, I was at my desk alone when a breathless John Murphy came hustling down the hall, waving a piece of paper. "You won't fucking believe it," he said as he put the paper in front of me. I looked down at a booking photo from a Dallas police station. There, looking straight out at me, holding a number across his chest, was James Hatfield.

"Oh crap, what was he busted for?" I asked.

Murphy replied, "Attempted murder. He put a pipe bomb in the tailpipe of his boss's car."

It is an odd sensation when everything shifts. One small picture lying on the desk, and every decision we had made became questionable.

I said, "Get me Hatfield, right now."

John bolted and then called from his office ten minutes later. "We can't find him."

"What in the hell do you mean you can't find him?"

"He appears to be gone."

The search began. He had checked out of his hotel. We called everyone we could think of; nobody had heard from Jim. He had vanished.

That afternoon it seemed like crow was on the menu. I took a large serving and dug in. We canceled the book. We issued a press release. We apologized profusely and repeatedly. We plowed through all the detail of recalling the book from the stores: it happens so rarely there is no playbook. And the book was selling even faster now. We decided we had to incentivize stores to send the books back, and we decided we had to chop them up when we got them. It was the right thing to do, and a financial disaster. At that moment it was probably good we couldn't find Jim.

A few days later Jim finally resurfaced. We canceled our contract and reverted the rights to *Fortunate Son* back to him. He sold the book again, unchanged, to Soft Skull Press. Jim stood by his story. A news show did a piece on the book, and later there was a documentary called *Horns and Halos*. Most of the movie was filmed in a gloomy basement of a New York apartment building where Soft Skull had a scattering of desks and phones. It was a setting as surreal as the story.

The last time I saw Jim he was trying to push the Soft Skull edition of *Fortunate Son* in our booth at a convention. He wanted to put a stack of marketing flyers on our reception desk, and I told him no. We talked a bit, and it was clear that he never stopped believing he had the story right. In frustration, that day he finally told me his source. He claimed it was Karl Rove, by then a senior advisor to President George W. Bush. Rove would eventually become the deputy chief of staff in the White House.

A few months later, Jim committed suicide.

It is impossible to know what happened back in the fall of 2000. There are clearly two likely scenarios. The first one is relatively simple. James Hatfield started to write his book using previously reported information. He uncovered some long-standing rumors and realized that if he used them as sourced reporting, he would have a much bigger book. He did a good job of it. We failed to recognize a pig in a poke, even when the elder President Bush warned us.

The second scenario is more complex. James Hatfield started digging around in Texas for information on the Republican nominee for the presidency. The Bush camp heard that Jim was out there digging, and while trying to block him, proceeded to do their own research. When they discovered that Jim had a criminal record, and that he was writing a quickie book on a short schedule, they saw an opportunity. There was no doubt that the cocaine rumor was out there, but maybe they could kill it. They leaked details of the cocaine bust (real or rumored) to Jim, from a credible source, Karl Rove. Jim ran with it, and we ran with it. And then, right before the book was published, they leaked the fact that the author was untrustworthy—in fact, a guy with a criminal record. The book died and the cocaine story died with it.

Many at St. Martin's Press came to believe the second scenario. It seemed to fit so well with Rove and the tactics he employed. It would have been a crafty and elegant solution to a difficult problem, perhaps a bit past ethical, but effective. And though Jim had clearly lied to us, he also believed deeply in the truth of his story.

Occam's Razor: the simplest explanation is usually right.

14.

Fast Cars and Meatloaf

J ANET EVANOVICH NEVER HESITATED TO CALL ME DIRECTLY. SHE had strong opinions, and she was happy to share them. That was fine with me; she was talented, hard-working, and extremely ambitious. Because of my job, I was the final "no" for many of her requests, and thus we had an uneasy personal relationship.

During a trip to Florida, I visited her house for a small celebratory party. She mentioned that she loved NASCAR, and I said I thought it was overrated as a spectator sport. This led to a spirited debate about driving in general, dirt tracks, and watching people drive in endless circles. I then confessed that I had never been to a major NASCAR event. She said that we needed to take care of that, and the conversation moved on. I thought nothing more of it.

The next week I got an email from Janet. The Darlington 500 was coming up, and she expected me to join her. She said she would pick me up in her plane. As her publisher, I thought I should probably pick her up in my plane. But I didn't have a plane, so I told her I would meet her in Darlington, and I booked a coach class ticket to Charleston. I figured if a guy was to go to NASCAR, he should take in a night of country music first and then drive at dawn across South Carolina.

On the assigned day I pulled into Darlington and picked up Janet and her daughter, Alex, at their motel. And it was a real motel, room doors facing the parking lot. In Darlington, luxury stops at the airport. We headed straight to the track to take in the pre-race activities. The first stop was a small trailer parked in a roped-off section of the lot, the temporary home office of Jim Hunter, the head of marketing for NASCAR. Jim was a good guy, and when Janet had to run to an appointment, he invited me to hang out with him. Twist my arm. We agreed to meet Janet at the drivers' meeting, and we headed off to the garages. We got to the area where they inspect cars, and we stopped to watch. I asked what they were looking for, and he explained that fractional tweaks in the mechanics could make a substantial difference in the outcome of the race. There is an ever-present temptation to adjust the car just a bit beyond the standards. Apparently, the honor system didn't work well, so every car gets an official once-over before the race.

I asked if we could join in on an inspection, which delighted Jim. He called over to the head of the inspection crew and asked. No problem. The inspector seemed to enjoy the company. First it was under the hood, then under the car. I was like a kid, pouring out a steady stream of stupid questions. No one seemed to mind.

As we walked back to the trailer Jim hailed a young guy coming the other way. "Hey, Mike, you got a minute to take John here for a ride?" Mike said he did. Jim asked, "John, you want to take a lap in the pace car?" Damn straight. We got in a regular-looking car, just me and Mike.

He apologized: "The car has been modified, but it doesn't go as fast as the race cars." I told him that was fine with me.

We buckled up, drove through the lot and down a small side road. There were people wandering about everywhere, and we wove through them. A small left turn, a guy opened a gate, and suddenly we were on the track. Darlington Speedway is longer than most, a roughly egg-shaped, 1.4-mile band of asphalt. The famous third turn is overly sharp and steep, a necessary distortion to protect a minnow pond the landowner admired when they built the place. The turn, and the track surface, are famously difficult and unpredictable. The track is known as "the Lady in Black" and scraping the paint off your car on the third turn wall is known as earning your Darlington stripe.

We started by going down the home stretch. The stands lined the track in front of us on the right, generally occupied, but still far from full. The track was empty. Stunningly empty. Mike looked over and caught my expression. "Do you want me to go as fast as I can?"

"Yes."

And then, after the stands flashed by on the right, "Do you want me to take the line the drivers use on the turns?"

"Oh yeah, please."

The lap happened quickly. It was all about the third turn. We entered the turn high up, the wall going by six inches from the car, a foot from my face. We slingshot down and left, the car shaking alarmingly on the rough road. Mike looked over and grinned. "Imagine doing that at full speed with a car a foot in front and a car a foot behind." It was hard to comprehend.

When we arrived back, Janet was done with her work. She had a book series that featured a NASCAR driver, so she was a bit of a celebrity among NASCAR folks. Today she planned to fill some airtime talking with the commentators in the booth, but for now we wandered through the packed concession stands on the way to the drivers' meeting. I bought a Dale Earnhardt Jr. #8 baseball cap for my son.

We arrived at a large tent, where the drivers sat at tables on plastic folding chairs. Race officials stood up front and went over details of the track, the pits, and the race rules. They discussed safety and they talked of the dangerous third turn. You could see the drivers nodding; they knew where the danger lived. As the meeting ended, Janet grabbed the cap from me and said that we needed to get it signed. I protested, let's not cause a stir. She gave me a very Janet look, grabbed my arm, and we were off to see Dale Jr. He happily signed the cap; they all loved Janet.

As race time approached, dark clouds rolled in. The radar offered bad news. The track blowers were readied, but there was little hope. We huddled under a small tent as the rain started. It appeared the race might never happen, but really, who cared. The main event was right there in the tent: homemade meatloaf sandwiches. Jim showed up and told stories. Now it was dumping buckets; the thunder boomed. I saw the meatloaf plate was empty. I opened the tent flap and ran to the cookhouse trailer. The guy said dinner was over, but I saw some meatloaf and convinced him to make another plate of sandwiches. I ran back to the tent through the rain and displayed my prize. It earned me high praise. "Hell, Janet, for a fancy New York publisher, this guy is alright."

Over the years Janet and I continued to have our differences, but the edge was gone. Meatloaf can solve lots of problems.

15.

The Problem with the Schmutz

THE WHITE HOUSE HAS A GREEN ROOM THAT IS ACTUALLY GREEN. It is a nice place, full of nice furniture, a room where you can wait for your chance to talk to people in the West Wing. There were four of us from Macmillan sitting in the green room, minding our own business, when three women arrived to put the final touches on the tree in the corner. It was a few weeks before the last Christmas of the Clinton administration, and the women were up from Arkansas to help with the decorating. They were in cheerful spirits, but they were clearly having a problem with the top of the tree. John Murphy and I wandered over and offered to help. John is a guy with lots of energy, and he likes laughter. The tree decorating turned into a boisterous affair. I climbed the ladder to the top, and was fully stretched out trying to attach the star, when Hillary Clinton's assistant arrived to say that the First Lady was ready to see us.

With John and me a bit disheveled, we were guided down the hall to another room with a couch and a circle of chairs. Hillary stepped in. We sat and talked about the book she wanted to write,

155

the book that would become *It Takes a Village*. It was a good meeting; she was friendly, and she answered every question directly. Her husband's impeachment trial had recently concluded, so we asked how it felt to give her testimony. She said the shame of it was completely overwhelming, and that she had struggled hard to hold it together. She said this with emotion, so I asked her how she managed to be so stoic in public. She told us that television amplifies emotion and that she knew even a single tear would cause her to look distraught. And she was determined not to look distraught.

We asked what she intended to write if she wasn't willing to express her emotions. She told us she could be emotional in a book because in writing you can control the level of the emotion on the page. She said that for her future in politics, she had to find a way to share her vulnerability with the American public. To accomplish that she would need to tell people honestly what she was feeling about her husband's affair. I remember thinking how remarkable that statement was, how remarkable she was, and that this book was going to be expensive.

Hillary's assistant stuck her head into the room. The meeting had run long, and Hillary was late for her upcoming speech. We all jumped up; there were hurried goodbyes. That is when I noticed something terribly wrong. Right before my eyes I saw it, there on the pocket of her jacket. Schmutz. It looked like a big glob of pink icing, lots of contrast against the tan of her pantsuit. She must have rubbed up against a cake before she came to see us.

Her handlers were waiting for her in the hall. She was going to a speech. Certainly, I should tell her about the schmutz on her pocket. Or should I? She was the First Lady. I struggled briefly with this overwhelming question and decided she must have someone who looked her over before the cameras came on. I swallowed my concern, and our goodbye was a "nice to meet you."

The woman who showed us out was the same woman who had busted us decorating the tree. She was very friendly, and as we walked down the hall she paused, looked around conspiratorially, and asked, "Hey, do you want to go out the long way and swing past the Oval Office?" Well sure, if you insist.

We walked down the famous hall, with the view of the breeze-way and a long row of Christmas trees lighting the night. The wind was strong; the flag on top of the Oval Office was horizontal in its spotlight. The president was in. As we passed his office, we could see that the door was shut. Two small groups of men huddled in chairs in front of the door. You could feel the intensity.

And then we were outside the fence, walking toward the cab stand. The White House was on our left, beaming in the brisk darkness. One of us said, "Sometimes, I just love my job." We all nodded our agreement.

The next week there was an auction for the book. Hillary knew that we had published *Monica's Story*, and it never entered the conversation. Much to her credit, she didn't care. When the auction finished, we were the underbidder. Just missed. We should have bid higher; *It Takes a Village* went on to sell millions of copies for S&S. Over the years, I occasionally thought about the schmutz, and my decision to stay silent. A decision of no consequence, made in an instant, and yet the memory remained.

Almost two decades later, in 2019, I went to a small party at Louise Penny's apartment. Louise is deeply interesting, like the characters in her novels. Her beloved husband Michael had passed away the year before, and in her struggle to move on she bought an apartment in New York City. It is a small space, beautifully designed by one of her pals. That night's party was to celebrate her new home with her New York friends. There were also a few of her fellow Canadians about, and she had done a very un-New York thing and invited her neighbors, the poor souls who had lived through the construction. It was a happy crowd, just the right number of people, cozy but not packed. The door opened one last time and in came Bill and Hillary

Clinton. Louise had made some interesting friends south of the border.

It is true what they say about Bill Clinton. He likes to focus in on a person and really talk. On this night, in front of the stove in Louise's kitchen, he chose me. He talked about the most recent election county by county; he didn't have many good things to say about the gerrymandering Republicans. We talked about sports. He talked about his book with James Patterson. But there, just ten feet away, was Hillary, the person who could answer my long-dormant question. An opportunity came, and I switched Clintons. We chatted a bit and then I came out with it. I told her about the schmutz and confessed that I had seen it and remained silent. Had I made the right decision? She laughed, looked at me like I was a bit odd, and said that it would indeed have been inappropriate to speak up. And yes, she did have someone who handled that sort of thing.

So now I know the answer. Some people have people who check for schmutz. If you see some on me, please speak up.

16.

9/11

ON SEPTEMBER 11, 2001, I WAS IN THE MACMILLAN OFFICES IN London. We were having a day of meetings to prepare for further meetings. After lunch, my colleague Mike Barnard slipped into the room while we were working. He bent over and whispered in my ear, "Do we have anyone in the World Trade Center?" I said no. He explained in a hushed voice that a plane had struck the building, and then exited the room as quietly as he had come. I imagined a small plane hitting the building, and then quickly returned my focus to the meeting. Moments later Mike was back, and he insisted we move down the hall to watch what was happening in New York on TV.

I remember watching with a sense of wonder. I was huddled in a small room full of Brits, while a mile from my house the world was changing. When the first building fell, I did the math on the time zones and realized with dread that Connie would be on the subway going to work. Her subway had a stop at Cortland Street, right underneath the World Trade Center. The TV news never mentioned the subway underneath the buildings that day, but I knew the news had to be bad.

I tried to call Connie with no success. All the circuits were down, and as time passed, my worry steadily increased. David Macmillan, who worked in our London office, stopped by and said he had reached some friends in Brooklyn. I asked him to call them back, and I gave him Connie's phone number and our address. I asked him if he would impose on his friends to go to my house. He rushed back to his office to try.

I was continuously dialing Connie, our house, and the office. I finally managed to reach someone at work. Thankfully all the people in our New York offices were safe, and they were evacuating the Flatiron Building due to its status as a landmark. Our employees were headed home. But still no word from Connie, and no news of our kids.

With the British stiff upper lip, we went back to work. Richard Charkin, the chief executive of Macmillan in the United Kingdom, loaned me his cell phone. I held it under the table, constantly hitting redial. We proceeded with a tedious review of financial statements and strategy documents; all the while I quietly dialed, my fear steadily compounding.

My chair in the conference room had a long view down the hall, offices on the left, workstations on the right. My eyes would wander there, looking for some sign. Suddenly I heard a yell at the far end of the building. Then David Macmillan burst into view, running, coming straight down the hall toward me. His hair was askew, his arm was waving in the air, and his hand was grasping his phone. And he was yelling, "I have found her! I've found her!" From the moment he had left me, for over an hour, David had been doing only one thing—constantly dialing, first his friend, then my wife.

Connie was fine. It was the first day of school; she had dropped the kids off late and had never gotten on the subway. I would fly on to Heidelberg. I would work in the strategy meetings all day, and then work the phones to the United States long into the night. Eventually I got the first flight from Europe into North America and hitchhiked home from Montreal. But my enduring memory of 9/11 has always been, and will always be, David's ecstatic running yell: "I've found her!"

17.

Finding Sandra

Tom McCormack, the former CEO of St. Martin's Press and the man who had originally recruited me, called me very early one April morning in 2006. He rarely called, and never outside normal office hours. When he spoke, the strain in his voice was palpable. Tom's wife, Sandra, was missing.

Sandra McCormack had been a senior editor at the company for decades, and in addition had served as its occasional interior decorator. She stayed on after Tom retired to read for other editors, and to edit a small list of her own. I took over her decorating responsibilities. In her final years at SMP she worked less and less as she struggled with the early stages of dementia. After she left the company, her dementia continued to worsen, and she reached the point of needing full-time care.

Tom and Sandra lived across the street from Central Park, and they often rode their bikes through its maze of roads and trails. The day before Tom's call they had gone to the park, a normal outing. They stopped to talk with someone, and for a moment Tom was too fully engaged in the conversation. Suddenly, Sandra was gone. Tom scoured the park and went to all the places they regularly visited. Getting more desperate, he called the police. As night fell, Sandra was still missing. Tom spent a sleepless night, and as the sky started to lighten, he called me for help.

I had grown up outside a small town. In small towns, when you need to find something, you just tell folks what you are looking for. That was generally accomplished by the posting of fliers, and it dawned on me that we could do that, even in New York City. I asked Tom for a recent photo of Sandra and a short description of her, including what she was wearing the day before.

As people started arriving at work, the company swung into gear. We asked for volunteers and our largest conference room began to fill. The art department designed a flier, and every copier in the building was pressed into emergency service printing them. We found and copied large-scale maps of the Upper West Side, from Central Park to the Hudson River. We calculated how many blocks a team of two could cover quickly, and we divided the maps into a grid. Each square of the grid was assigned a number, with a search team to cover it.

Helen Plog, who managed office services at the company for fifty-three years, came up with dozens of staplers and endless rolls of tape. We set up a small command center to monitor the phone number on the flier and to track the search teams. By 9:30 a.m. the conference room was full, people had their assigned square on the grid, and copies of the flier were flowing from every corner of the building. We deployed to the subways. Fliers went up, two per block on every street. And they went up fast. We stapled or taped them on any surface where they could be seen, and all our eyes were peeled for Sandra.

I swung by Tom's house to fill him in on our progress and then departed to my assigned grid square, a section of Central Park. I was walking the roads putting up fliers and searching the small trails for any clue that might lead to Sandra. I was in a clump of trees when I was startled to hear my borrowed phone ringing. Sandra had been found. A staffer at the ABC studios on 66th Street had gone out for a morning coffee at Starbucks. She saw a flier and after walking across the street, she saw a woman who looked familiar sitting on a bench. She went back to check the flier and called the number. The command center called the team assigned to the grid square, and they ran two blocks to the bench. Sandra was sitting there, quietly.

Tom sent out her nurse to bring her home. All the searchers retraced their steps, taking down the fliers. Sandra had been taken in by a friendly soul the night before and was in a cheerful mood after her big adventure. We'll never know why she wandered off, nor what she did in those twenty hours. But at the heart of the story there was a kind stranger.

We were at our best that morning.

18.

A Good Ride

IT WAS SUMMERTIME IN WYOMING. CONNIE, KYLE, JACK, AND I
were out for our annual visit to see my mother at the ranch. The
first morning we gathered at the breakfast table to plan the many
events that would fill our days. Much to my surprise, this year the
kids wanted to go horseback riding.

Growing up I rode a lot, mostly checking fence lines and counting cattle. But horses and I had a difficult relationship. Starting
when I was little, I had a big gray named Smokey Joe. He didn't
like me much. After a while, I didn't like him much either, but we
had work to do together. I fed and brushed him, he mostly tried to
step on my feet or kick me, often successfully. He had to carry me
around, which was probably unpleasant, but I thought he crossed a
line that time he bit me. I rode Smokey Joe for ten years. He never
stopped trying to get the better of me, and I never knew how to
stop him.

Smokey Joe was long gone at this point, but there were always
horses on the ranch. We used to take the kids riding every summer,

but as they grew older, we only went riding when they wanted to. In recent years they hadn't asked, and I wasn't heartbroken. But this summer horses were back on the activity list, so we chose a day.

At the appointed hour, Kathy Daly, who manages Mom's place, reported that we were down to four horses. As we got ready to go, she took me aside to say the new bay had been acting widgy, and it would probably be best if I rode him.

We went out and got the horses, then saddled up. The bay was calm as I tightened the cinch, no bloating, no trickery. We had a nice ride, just a short trip over the hills behind the house. The horses walked in their line, swishing tails, the smell of leather, a gentle rocking in the saddle. It had been a wet spring and the grass was high, the air smelled of sage, and the distant peaks were covered in winter's snow. As the sun warmed toward noon, we headed back to the arena. There was still no sign of widginess from the bay. He was a strong quarter horse, alert and responsive.[7] I thought it a shame that he hadn't had a chance to run.

I was curious to see how fast this horse could go, so I rode him to the fence and turned him to face the open arena. I reined him in; he backed to the fence and tensed. He knew what was coming. I leaned forward, delivered a hard kick, and gave him his head. I probably made one of those classic western noises: *Heeyaa*.

The best part of riding is the initial burst of acceleration. All that coiled energy suddenly releases when the horse lunges forward. The ears flatten; the nostrils flare. You can feel the muscles. This horse did not disappoint. He hurled himself forward as I leaned over his neck. Here we go. And then he locked his front

---

7   The American Quarter Horse got its name for its great speed at short distances, particularly the quarter mile. The horse is also extremely quick and agile, perfectly suited for working cattle. They are known for their broad chests and powerful hindquarters; their top speed is 44 mph.

knees, dug in, and bucked. I was still going up when I passed over his head.

Time slowed. I considered that my feet were now traveling above me. Upside down, I thought about what it could mean, and I managed to form a full sentence in my head: *Oh shit, this is gonna hurt.* Then time ran out, and I landed flat on my back. There was pain. I was frozen for a moment, stunned, and struggling to get air into my lungs. As my breath returned, I lay in the arena dirt and checked my parts. They all seemed to function. I remained still, feeling the dirt under my back and gazing at the sky. Then I got up, dusted off, and got back on the horse. Always get back on the horse. The kids were wide-eyed when I rode up; alarmed for me and for themselves.

Riding never made it back on the activities list in the years ahead. But that was a great day: the four of us together, the rhythm of the horses, and the long mountain views. There was some adrenaline spent, a chance taken, and a moment of dangerous consequence. It was a good ride.

19.

Nobody Wins Afraid of Losing

Eddy Comes to Town

The fight would last for more than eight years. It would end at
the doors of the Supreme Court, with the world's most valuable
corporation squared off against the Department of Justice. On
November 19, 2007, in Manhattan, Jeff Bezos of Amazon threw
the first punch. I had a ringside seat that day.

The first Kindle ebook reader was an odd wedge-shaped device
with small, hard-to-operate buttons. Amazon had shown us pro-
totypes during its development, and we told them we thought the
shopping experience was good, but the device was not. Eventually,
we agreed to sell Macmillan ebooks on Kindle, on the same terms
as printed books. In the fall of 2007, I got an invitation to an
Amazon press conference where they would launch the device.
They called to tell me that Jeff was personally asking me to attend.

I agreed to go, and so on November 19, I made my way to the
W Hotel near Union Square, expecting the usual Amazon no-frills

gathering. Instead, they had rented a ballroom and put in a stage. There was a screen so large that the room looked small; it felt more like Apple than Amazon. They showed me to a reserved seat in the front row. Looking right I saw some of the brass from the other big publishers; so much for being special. Bezos ran up onto the stage holding a Kindle. He discussed all the features and boldly stated that over 90 percent of the current *New York Times* bestseller list would be available. And then he threw his punch.

He stood in front of the publishers and, without making eye contact, said the Kindle ebook price for all hardcover bestsellers would be $9.99. He was planning to sell our best books for less than he paid for them, and for more than 60 percent off the hardcover price. And he hadn't even bothered to tell us before he told the world.

Lots of people began to buy the device. In October 2008, Jeff went on *Oprah* to talk about ebooks. At the end of the show Oprah encouraged her viewers to buy a Kindle, stressing the $9.99 price point of the books.

At about that time, there was a dinner at a "fancy midtown restaurant" named Picholine. It was a dinner to welcome Markus Dohle, the new Random House CEO, to the publishing industry and to the United States. It was a well-meant and kind gesture. But it was the CEOs of all the big publishers, together in a private room. A private room in the back. It wasn't just a private room in the back either; it was called the Chef's Wine Cellar. The walls of the room were racks of expensive bottles of wine. It barely held us all, and a waiter stood outside the door, waiting to be called in. The food was good, and the conversation was harmless. It wasn't a conspiracy as it was later described, but if it had been, the setting would have been perfect.

On February 10, 2009, Amazon released Kindle 2; there was no more wedge shape, no more annoying buttons, and Oprah had given her blessing. Now lots and lots of people were buying

Kindles, and sales of low-priced ebooks grew exponentially. In March, I flew to Seattle and spent a day talking about business models with Amazon. Both sides had been extensively coached by lawyers about words that could not be used. We spent tense hours describing what problems we had in our respective business models, in a sort of made-up business gibberish that tiptoed around the issue of the $9.99 price point. It was a legally correct conversation, a good effort on both sides, but it was to no avail.

Publishers constantly tried to figure out how to stop the steep decline in the price of new books, driven by Amazon's pricing of ebooks. If readers started to believe the right price for an author's bestselling new work was less than ten bucks, many industry executives feared the ecosystem of publishing would collapse. The problem kept getting worse, particularly after the launch of Kindle 2. At Macmillan we studied all the possible options and found none we thought would work, except for not selling Amazon the books in the first place. We began to window (delay the publication of the ebook format until after the hardcover) select titles as a test. Other publishers must have felt the same, because by December 2009 several large publishers announced plans to window across their lists.

At this point Barnes & Noble had the Nook, and Indigo was developing the Kobo, but we knew that neither would have the muscle to take on Amazon in the long run. What we needed was a serious technology player in the game. We needed Apple. Earlier in 2009 I had called Rob McDonald, our contact at Apple for audiobooks. I had asked him who I could talk to at Apple about ebook. He had said that would be Eddy Cue. When I asked for Eddy's contact information, Rob just laughed. "That's not the way it works. If Eddy wants to talk to you, he will call you," A bit annoyed, I googled Eddy Cue. The search result described Eddy's new title at Apple as "The Lord God of Awesomeness." Properly intimidated, I didn't call.

In the last months of 2009, the problem kept getting worse. Amazon was now responsible for 90 percent of our ebook sales, most at the damaging low price. Retail sales in bookstores were dropping. At Macmillan, we debated constantly if brick and mortar bookstores could survive. We had seen what happened with record stores and the music industry, and it was clear that we might be on the same path. Agents and authors were pushing for higher ebook royalties and rightfully worrying about their future income. If a new book was only worth ten bucks, how would they make a living? There were conversations with Amazon, the Author's Guild, agents, authors, and booksellers. All these conversations would be scrutinized by teams of lawyers in the years ahead.

Ebook pricing was in the press constantly. It became much of my job, a lens through which we viewed every decision. If the survival of the business was not at stake, it certainly felt like it was. We had to find a way to control the price. And then on Friday, December 11, 2009, the phone rang on my desk. "Hi John, my name is Eddy Cue and I work at Apple." I reported that I knew who he was. Eddy might be the Lord God of Awesomeness, but he sounded like a nice guy. He said he was coming to town, and would I have time to talk? I suppressed my urge to yell "Oh hell yeah!" We set a date.

Eddy carries his confidence easily, and he clearly enjoys the Apple mystique. He told us that Apple might or might not be making a new device; it was too secret to discuss. If there was a new device, it might have an ebook store on it; it might not. He told us Random House, the largest American publisher, would not agree to be in the store, if there was a store. But he reported with a serious tone that if he could get four of the other five big publishers to agree to terms in the next few weeks, there would probably be a bookstore—if, of course, there was a device. There was a firm date for when the deal had to be done—if there was a deal to be done.

Eddy went from publisher to publisher offering a new business model based on what Apple used for iTunes and the App Store. The new deal, called the agency model, would allow each publisher to control the price of their products. Publishers would set the price of their ebooks and the retailers, as their agents, would get a percentage of that price. Eddy was relentless but endlessly cheerful in his pursuit. He identified other publishers by number only: "I had some success with publisher number two on this point." We tried to get him to say something that would give us a hint about which publisher he was referring to. If he said he was going to see publisher number three next, we would try to get him to slip and say "him" or "her" when talking about the CEO, or to say he was going uptown or downtown to his next meeting. He never slipped, never gave us a clue. We could never determine who was in and who was out.

Negotiations continued over the Christmas break. I was staying out on Long Island with my family and a blizzard dropped a couple feet of drifting snow. A day passed and no snowplows showed up. Time was getting short, and I needed to get back to town. We live a quarter mile down a small road, but I decided to dig us out. I borrowed my son's cellphone so I would be able to make a scheduled call to Eddy without coming back to the house. After eleven hours of shoveling through the afternoon and the following morning, I had fashioned a ragged path through the drifts, and we drove home.

Eddy came to town a second time for another round of negotiating. On Thursday, January 20, Eddy confessed the deadline was driven by Steve Jobs's dress rehearsal for the new product launch. If there was a bookstore, it would be featured. If there wasn't a bookstore, it would be deleted from the script before the rehearsal. The stop date was one day away. We were down to a couple of contract points, and Eddy said he had two publishers committed. He called me that afternoon. He said he had talked to Steve, and they had agreed to go forward with fewer than the four publishers they had initially required, but one of them had to be Macmillan, specifically me. He said that our meeting the next day was going to be great, followed by "We have to be all done by tomorrow afternoon. So tomorrow morning, John, you get to decide if Apple builds a bookstore." No pressure, mind you.

Over the previous few years, a group of eight senior managers at Macmillan met weekly to discuss digital changes in the book industry and the issues we faced. We tried to always make the big decisions together. Now, on Thursday afternoon, we gathered, and I asked them for advice about changing to the agency model. At the end of the discussion, I put it to a vote. The vote was split.

The next morning, Friday, at 4:00 a.m., I got on the exercise bike in my basement. I cleared my head and thought about the decision I needed to make. I thought about the right decision-making process and what factors I should consider. And then I began to think through all the issues. I remember a brief intensity, and then, in a few short minutes, I had an answer.

Later that morning, Eddy came by the Flatiron for our negotiation; security downstairs announced his arrival. Brian Napack, Macmillan's president, and I were waiting in my office. The phone rang. To my amazement it was Brian Murray, the CEO of Harper Collins. As he started to talk, I saw Eddy walking down the hall to my office. Napack was on his game. He jumped up and rushed out to block Eddy with friendly small talk. Murray told me he felt he had to call, and that he was not going forward with Apple. Brian and I often talked about AAP matters and joint ventures, but this was the first and only time we talked about the agency model. Since he was not going forward, it was a legal call. And it was also seriously bad news. The call meant the two largest publishers, Random and Harper, were out. It also meant the two publishers that Eddy had signed up for the agency model were smaller publishers, and that there was one publisher who was either out or sitting on the fence. I was completely uncertain if the new business model could even get started with that level of support.

I stood to greet Eddy and Kevin Saul, the Apple lawyer on the deal. We sat and began to haggle the remaining contract points. Finally, in exasperation, I asked, "How can you come in here for these negotiations, make all these demands, show no flexibility, say no to everything we ask for, and meanwhile not even tell us if you will have a new device, never mind a new store?"

Eddie leaned back in his chair, completely relaxed, gave me a smile, and said, "Because we are Apple." On the very last point Eddy gave in. It was a small point.

After our handshake, Eddy told me he was going to spend the weekend in New York to get the deal done. "I'm not leaving town without signed papers." I asked him if he was going to watch the football playoffs alone in his hotel room. Yes, he was. I told him that was just too depressing; he should come watch at my house. He did, and we had a great afternoon. My son loved Eddy, and when I told him that Eddy was in charge of iTunes, Jack was slack-jawed. There was another *dad is cool* moment.

We signed the deal on Monday. Eddie told me he thought he would get two more publishers before his flight home, and he invited me out to California to see the launch of the new device. He tempted me with "We can hang out with Steve." As fun as that sounded, I knew I had to go to Seattle instead. Amazon was our largest customer, and they deserved to hear the news about the agency model from me in person. I suspected it would not go well.

Bet the Ranch

Apple announced the new device on Wednesday, January 27. Steve Jobs launched the iPad, and he featured the new bookstore in his demo. Unfortunately, in answering a question, he said the price for ebooks on the iPad would be the same as on the Kindle and all the other devices. It was true because each agency publisher would now determine what would be charged for their ebooks, but his statement would lead us down a long and difficult road. The next morning, Brian Napack and I boarded a plane for Seattle. At the time, Amazon headquarters was in the PacMed building, an old twelve-story hospital just up the hill from Interstate 5 on the way into town. Our flight had been late, and I was driving faster than might be advised. As we sped up the driveway a black dog ran out in front of the car. I swerved and hit the brakes. Brian said, "Jesus, don't start things off by running over Jeff's dog."

As usual at Amazon, we were led to a conference room for the meeting. Brian and I sat on one side of the table. Russ Grandinetti, Laura Porco, and David Naggar, the three senior Amazon executives in charge of books, sat on the other. Steve Kessel, the guy responsible for all things Kindle, sat at the end of the table on our left. It was tense from the moment we walked in. There was no small talk except for our attempted humor about almost hitting Jeff's dog. They didn't appear to think it was funny. I told them we had come out to have a difficult conversation face to face, and that we understood they might want us to head right back to the airport. I told them that we were moving to agency terms. They were decidedly unhappy. I told them they could stay on their old terms, but we would not sell them new books upon publication. This led to a stony stare and a short question, "How long will we have to wait?" There was a second or two of silence; I steeled myself and said, "Seven months."

Steve's face reddened, and I could see a vein pulsing in Russ's forehead as he asked harshly, "What the hell do you expect us to say to that?" David laced into us with vigor. Steve added a comment or two. I made it clear that we had no flexibility. They told us it might be best for us to go back to the airport.

Russ led us out to reception. We were walking down a wide hallway three abreast, in silence. Russ finally said, "Look around, guys; this is the last time you will ever be in this building." My step faltered; I couldn't believe he would say that. Russ looked over and saw our expressions. He looked puzzled for a second and then it dawned on him. "Guys, we are moving to a new building in a few weeks. I didn't mean you could never come back to Amazon." That story took on a life of its own, and for years Amazon newbies would ask, "Are you one of the guys Russ threw out of the building?"

Brian and I loaded into the car and drove into Seattle, ever on the alert for the dog. We talked about what would come next. As we pulled up to a stop sign near Pioneer Square, Brian asked if I thought they might pull the buy buttons from our titles. I told him I was pretty sure they wouldn't; it was the nuclear option, a very public display of their power to intimidate, and I didn't think it made sense. He agreed. Brian flew home that night, and I went to dinner with some old friends; they never suspected their email exchange with me from that afternoon would be shown in federal court.

The next day, I flew home. When the plane landed on Friday night, I had two emails of note. One was from Richard Sarnoff saying he thought his company, Random House, had made a mistake by not going agency. That gave me some relief, as I admired Richard and could not imagine that he had been a believer in Random House's decision. The second was from Russ: "Please call as soon as you can." The cab dropped me at my front door; I walked into the kitchen and dialed Russ.

He got straight to the point. "We are taking the buy buttons down on all Macmillan titles." I asked if that included all trade titles. "Yes." Children's books? "Yes." Scholarly and reference? "Yes." Higher education textbooks? "Yes." Distributed lines? "Yes." Just Kindle or physical books as well? "Everything."

I convinced him not to punish our distributed publishers, and then asked, "When do you plan to do it?"

He responded, "We just did." He asked that we keep the dispute between us, not in the press. I agreed. We hung up, and I checked the Amazon site. Sure enough, the buy buttons were down on Macmillan's books.

Alarmed, but already late, I ran out to meet Connie at a friend's house for dinner. Walking down the street, I realized that we were in deep trouble. That was quickly followed by a more self-centered thought: I was going to be working all weekend. At dinner, some of the people had already heard the Amazon news and were riled up. It dawned on me that I was underestimating the scope of the problems we would be facing.

Late that night, I pondered how to get around the media silence that is usually honored between publishers and their retail accounts. I realized I had agreed with Russ too quickly not to go to the press. I knew this would be a PR game, and that public opinion would rule the day. I knew that Amazon always put their customers first, and the public was their customer. But how could we get the story out? The answer, when it came to me, was simple. The next morning, I went into the Flatiron. Macmillan occupied the whole building at this point, and it appeared to be completely empty on that winter Saturday. There was the desk guy downstairs but otherwise I sat in the old triangular landmark alone.

That feeling of being alone was going to be the key to the whole thing. A seemingly small publisher against a massive retailer. David vs. Goliath. The speed and broad scope of Amazon's actions provided the dynamic we would need. They were damaging us, and they were damaging authors. They were ruthless. Our response would come from me, a single voice, not an announcement from a corporation.

I emailed Russ and told him that since he had taken the buttons down so quickly, we had to explain the situation to our authors. They were hugely affected by Amazon's actions, and there was no way to reach them quickly on a Saturday without using the press. He agreed; I don't think he had much choice. I wrote a letter to our authors, to be delivered through the press, trying to walk a very fine line between respect and determination. I sent it to others at Macmillan for their review.

We had never hired a director of communications at Macmillan; I filled that role whenever it was needed. It was needed now. I called Michael Cader, who nine years earlier had started *Publishers Lunch*, a publishing newsletter that I admired. I asked him if he would run a Saturday edition. We would pay for it by booking ad space, and the ad would be the letter to our authors. Michael agreed and gave me a great price to boot. I sent a draft of my letter to the *Wall Street Journal* and the *New York Times* and told them they could not publish anything until they saw the story go up on *Publishers Lunch*. Michael gave up his Saturday and wrote an article to go with the letter. He also afforded me a much-needed copyedit and formatted my writing to make it look reasonably professional.

He sent me back the formatted letter and said it would go up the minute I gave him the green light. I read it again. And yet again. And then again. I typed "good to go" in a reply to Michael. Then I read the whole thing again. I took a deep breath and hit send.

Almost immediately I got the *Publishers Lunch* newsletter in my inbox. The formatting on my letter was superb. The next two emails, seconds later, were the *WSJ* and the *Times* stories. And then a remarkable thing happened. My email screen filled so fast it began to move. And it didn't stop. One came from Switzerland: "I just heard the news on the radio." I sat at the top of the Flatiron, in silent wonder, watching my screen scroll all by itself.

Saturday night and Sunday morning the support flowed in. It came from all corners of the globe and all corners of the business. There were some intensely negative words on the tech blogs, and *Business Insider* led with the provocative headline, "Hey John Sargent, Screw You." The mainstream media, though, following the *Times* and the *WSJ*, tended to side with Macmillan and the authors against the might of Amazon. There were stories everywhere, in some cases lead stories and front-page headlines. The outpouring from authors, agents, and publishers was hugely positive. I was back at my desk all day Sunday, managing email, planning the next steps, and communicating with authors and agents. After that first letter, Macmillan was resolutely silent in the press.

Early Sunday afternoon, I got a call from Amazon that they were going to post something. Later, I got an email from the *Times* reporter with a link to a Kindle Community forum. And there it was in the second paragraph: "We want you to know that ultimately, however, we will have to capitulate and accept Macmillan's terms because Macmillan has a monopoly over their own titles . . ."

There is a theory that raising your arms is a universal human reaction of celebration. It happened to me, on a Sunday afternoon sitting in front of a computer screen. The elation was soon replaced by an overwhelming flood of relief.

On the day before, I had scheduled a Monday morning meeting with all the publishers and editors to discuss how we would communicate with authors and agents. We didn't have a room big enough, so we emptied a conference room in the point of the Flatiron and filled it with chairs. I was a few minutes late and the place was packed when I walked in. They all stood with a mighty roar. OK, maybe it wasn't a mighty roar, but it sure felt that way. I told them that we could not crow, we could not claim victory. There was still a tremendous amount of work to do, and Amazon had to be respected by all of us. Just hours later the hard work began.

Amazon demanded that we negotiate a new contract before they would sell Macmillan books again. The contract would be under agency terms of sale, so it would have to be created from scratch. We would try to do it in under a week, though a simple contract update with Amazon generally took a couple of months at the minimum. Russ and I set to the task. By Monday afternoon, Amazon's stock price was plunging and phone calls poured in from anxious authors and agents. The pressure started to mount. There was a front-page article in the *Wall Street Journal* with the quote, "The future of e-books, the future of publishers' control over their own destiny, and the future of retail pricing is being forged right before our eyes."

The work was hugely challenging. There were large conceptual issues—how do you structure a contract to prevent discounting, on a website built on the premise of discounting? And there was daunting detail, new legal concepts constructed sentence by sentence, word by word, comma by comma. Any concession we gave to Amazon would be a concession forever. And we understood that it would not be just a Macmillan contract; Amazon would make the basic terms an industry standard.

We started negotiating every day at 6:00 a.m. Seattle time and ended around 9:00 p.m. New York time. Russ was grumpy to get in so early, and I was grumpy to stay so late. Every few hours we would take a break. Russ would go talk to Bezos, lawyers, and others at Amazon, and I would gather small groups of advisors at Macmillan. I had always kept my office door open, but now I sat in my office behind a closed door, talking on the phone with Russ or thinking through what to do next.

Spontaneously, booksellers across the country moved Macmillan titles to the front of their stores. In some malls they put out kiosks of Macmillan books. When we asked our accounts for help, they helped. Agents called with questions, but they were mostly supportive. A few asked, "John, we support you 100 percent but couldn't we make an exception for my author's new book?" Amazon's stock price kept going down. Authors continued to worry. The publishing world waited.

Every day I would take a quick break for lunch at the deli across the street. On Tuesday when I got back, there was a seven-foot-tall Louisville Slugger baseball bat in my office, casually leaning in a corner. I knew it normally stood in Matthew Shear's office, three floors below mine, but there was no note, just the bat. The next day there was an old WPA axe. And then brass knuckles. A meat tenderizer. Another axe, this one with a nasty hooked blade. Boxing gloves. A knife. Whenever I left my office, I would come back to find a new weapon, randomly placed by unidentified Macmillan employees.

On Tuesday afternoon, Steve Rubin, the publisher of Holt, appeared at my door. He was jubilant, waving a proof of a full-page ad in the *New York Times*. It would run the next day to promote Atul Gawande's new book, *The Checklist Manifesto*. Added to the usual language of "Available in Bookstores Everywhere" were two words: "Except Amazon." Atul had bravely approved the wording, a risk most authors would be loath to take. I tried to be enthusiastic. When Steve left, I called Russ and told him what to expect the next morning in the *Times*. His response was blunt. "Are you fucking kidding me? Do you have any clue how high the emotions are out here? You need to stop it." We tried to stop it, but the *Times* was already on press.

Early Wednesday morning Connie informed me that my hair was turning gray. When I went back to the bathroom and looked in the mirror, I saw that she was right. Aging overnight. By Thursday the contract was close to finished, but we had pushed off the toughest two points. That afternoon we reached a total impasse. Russ refused to budge and so did I. We got off the phone, and he went to talk it over with his powers that be. When he called back, he was resolute, and so was I. He said the buy buttons would stay off. I asked, "How long?"

He replied "Forever."

I responded "So be it" and hung up the phone.

I jumped out of my chair and walked furiously in small circles around my office. Small circles are very small in an office shaped like a triangle. Christ, what had I done? We would not last a year without Amazon as a customer. I sat back down, and I stood back up. I paced some more. A half hour later when the phone rang, I snatched it up. It was Russ. He offered a startling solution, something so out of the box and yet so simple that it was hard to grasp for a moment. But I could see that with some small changes it would work. I marveled, yet again, at the boldness and intelligence of the folks at Amazon. On Friday we signed a contract, an hour shy of one week from the moment they turned the buy buttons off. By Saturday it was back to business as usual; the new contract would go into effect in April when the iPad became available.

A few weeks later I got a call from Eddy. He was coming to town; would I meet him for lunch? And since I had missed the show in California, would I like to see an iPad prototype? We went out for burgers, and he set up our menus to form a make-shift wall. He reached into his bag and pulled out the device that Apple had indeed built, and he showed me the bookstore. It was a remarkable moment, seeing the ballyhooed device and getting a tour of the features from Eddy. The waitress came over and caught a glimpse. She asked in amazement, "Is that one of those new iPad thingees everyone is talking about?" The thingee went back in Eddy's bag in a flash, and the failed menu walls came down. Eddy told me he had a story I would like. He recounted sitting in his office and reading the letter I wrote to the authors when Amazon took down our buy buttons. He told me he printed a copy and walked over to Steve Jobs's office, handed it to Steve, and said, read this, you will love it. Steve read the letter, looked up, and said, "This guy is gonna kick Amazon's ass." Eddy is a charming guy, and he might have embellished a bit, but I choose to believe every word was true.

I became briefly famous in the world of books. There had been lots of press in Europe; they were naturally against Amazon and supportive of publishers. The newspaper stories there were more colorful; in France I was called the cowboy publisher. Amazon was just entering the Italian market and publishers there started calling to ask my advice. One of them, Stefano Mauri, commissioned a rendering of me as Che Guevara, had it printed on buttons, and proposed giving them out at the Frankfurt Book Fair. Thankfully he agreed not to. I got an award from the New Zealand publishers, which they presented to me in my office. In the United States, booksellers I would meet would often hug me, usually after saying, "You're John Sargent?" I guess I never looked the part. At the University of Colorado where my daughter was taking a class in current events, the professor suggested they talk about Amazon and Macmillan and he mentioned this guy Sargent. Even at work, when I stepped in the elevator, people would look at me differently.

A few months later, as things were approaching normal, Wu Shu Linn, the true power behind all aspects of publishing in China, asked for a meeting to discuss ebooks. He came to my office with an assistant, a translator, and a British advisor. We talked about reading devices, ebooks, the Chinese market, and Amazon. Toward the end, he brought up his recent trip to Iceland, and this led us to his love of fishing. We moved on to discuss our mutual admiration of mountains. I told him I grew up at the foot of the Rockies. He exclaimed, "I love the Rocky Mountains!" I asked why and he said, "The music! John Denver!"

I hesitated for a second, then thought *what the heck*, and started to sing, "Almost heaven, West Virginia . . ."

Startled, he hesitated, and then he sang back, "Blue Ridge Mountains, Shenandoah River . . ." Thankfully his voice was as bad as mine. We did the first verse of "Country Roads" alternating lines, and we sang the chorus together. His entourage sat wide eyed, their mouths gaping open. Then he burst into laughter, rushed over, gave me a big hug, and insisted that I come to stay at his house. Ever since then, when people come back from conferences in China, they call me and say Wu Shu Linn sends his regards. That meeting felt like the final surreal moment.

But then things got stranger.

Lawyer Up

The iPad launched successfully, but the Apple bookstore was hurt by a lack of selection. Harper Collins went agency after Steve Jobs went directly to James Murdoch at Fox, Harper's parent company. Penguin finally went agency as well, but Random House, the largest publisher, didn't change terms for a year and did not sell ebooks through Apple. And thus, Amazon's Kindle continued to dominate.

All along there was another stew brewing. Even as Russ and I were negotiating with the buy buttons down, Amazon lawyers were preparing an antitrust complaint to the FTC. On February 1, 2010, Amazon also sent a white paper to the DOJ explaining why they felt antitrust laws had been violated. Through various channels, they encouraged the US government and the state of Texas to investigate the publishing industry's change to agency terms. Amazon would argue that Apple and the publishers colluded illegally to try to raise prices.

Shortly thereafter, we got a call from the Department of Justice. They requested a conversation with me, more chat than interrogation. We agreed and I showed up with three lawyers. They had lots more lawyers. The lead lawyer from the DOJ seemed like a nice guy; it was all very polite. After it was over, he came up to me and said that he had read a lot of what I had written, and there was one thing that impressed him greatly. I was all puffed up and trying to think which email of genius he might be referring to when he asked, "Did you really shovel snow for a quarter mile? By hand?"

I could not imagine that there was a case for the DOJ. Amazon had dominant market share, over 90 percent at the time, and Apple was a new entrant in the market. I was amazed when Joel Mitnick, our outside antitrust attorney, reported that the DOJ and Texas planned to file against Apple and the five publishers who had switched to agency terms. The DOJ informed us they were going to announce the lawsuit, and they asked us to settle. We declined. They came back shortly thereafter and told us three of the other publishers had already agreed to settle, and they were adamant that we should follow suit. They threatened that if we did not agree to settle now, Macmillan would be heavily featured in the filing. Again, we declined.

On April 10, 2012, the day before the announcement, Joel called me to deliver a message from the DOJ: "Tell Mr. Sargent that if he does not settle today, we will come after him personally."

I told Joel he could give them a message back: "Fuck you." Joel, in his calm way, informed me that he would not advise using that sort of language with the DOJ. I asked that he use whatever language he thought best.

That night Joel called me at home. Eric Holder, the attorney general of the United States, would announce the lawsuit at a live press conference the next morning. Joel suggested I brace myself because Holder would be referring to me personally as a bad actor. That night I wrote my family to warn them, and to assure them that I was innocent. I also wrote another letter:

Dear authors, illustrators and agents:

Today the Department of Justice filed a lawsuit against Macmillan's US trade publishing operation, charging us with collusion in the implementation of the agency model for ebook pricing. The charge is civil, not criminal. Let me start by saying Macmillan did not act illegally. Macmillan did not collude.

We have been in discussion with the Department of Justice for months. It is always better, if possible, to settle these matters before a case is brought. The cost of continuing—in time, distraction, and expense—are truly daunting.

But the terms the DOJ demanded were too onerous. After careful consideration, we came to the conclusion that the terms could have allowed Amazon to recover the monopoly position it had been building before our switch to the agency model. We also felt the settlement the DOJ wanted to impose would have a very negative impact on those who sell books for a living, from the largest chain stores to the smallest independents.

When Macmillan changed to the agency model we did so knowing that we would make less money on our ebook business. We made the change to support an open and competitive market for the future, and it worked. We still believe in that future, and we still believe the agency model is the only way to get there.

It is also hard to settle a lawsuit when you know you have done no wrong. The government's charge is that Macmillan's CEO colluded with other CEOs in changing to the agency model. I am Macmillan's CEO, and I made the decision to move Macmillan to the agency model. After days of thought and worry, I made the decision on January 22, 2010 a little after 4:00 a.m., on an exercise bike in my basement. It remains the loneliest decision I have ever made, and I see no reason to go back on it now.

Other publishers have chosen to settle. That is their decision to make. We have decided to fight this in court. Because others have settled, there may well be a preponderance of references to Macmillan, and to me personally, in the Justice Department's papers—often without regard to context. So be it.

I hope you will agree with our stance, and with Scott Turow, the president of the Author's Guild, who stated, "The irony of this bites hard: our government may be on the verge of killing real competition in order to save the appearance of competition. This would be tragic for all of us who value books and the culture they support."

Since we are now in litigation, I may not be able to comment much going forward. We remain dedicated to finding the best long-term outcome for the book business, for Macmillan and for the work you have entrusted to our care.

Thanks.

We rushed to release the letter to the press early the next morning. The government pushed back their press conference by a few hours, which allowed us to get our side of the story out first. By the time the attorney general spoke, the articles in the press were half written, and we fared well.[8]

The lawsuit was colossal. We were being sued by the United States, thirty-three individual states, and twenty-six consolidated class action law firms. The European Union and Canada piled on a bit later. The case moved forward with daunting amounts of discovery and an endless string of sworn depositions. At Macmillan several executives were deposed. I took on the role of representing the company in the depositions, as well as being deposed separately in my role as CEO.

The day came for my first deposition training session at Sidley Austin's New York office. Joel met us at reception. I was with Amy Wolosoff and Paul Sleven, the two Macmillan lawyers who would be constant companions in the months ahead. Joel, already a fixture in my life, led us to a long conference room filled with a high-gloss table and a multitude of chairs. There were four or five Sidley lawyers seated on the far side of the table. Running down the center of the tabletop, all the way from one end to the other, was a line of black four-ring binders, each one four to five inches thick. Joel waved his arm theatrically. "This is your email." Then he placed his hand on the binder at the head of the table, noticeably thicker than all the others, and spun it to show me the label. The label said CSARGENT@EARTHLINK.NET, and Joel said,

---

8   Months later I was told why the government made the sudden change from a press release to a live press conference by Eric Holder. The night before, Mitt Romney had been identified as the presumptive Republican challenger to President Obama. Apple had just become the most valuable company on earth. The United States government going after Apple would grab some of the front-page headlines away from Romney. If the story was true, the strategy worked.

"And this is a problem. You have got to stop emailing your wife." I had never realized that emailing legal correspondence to Connie would exempt the emails from attorney/client privilege.

The rehearsals were endless. Joel pretended to be the DOJ lawyer, and he was nasty. He hammered at me on all the points he thought they would use against us. Joel discussed strategy and explained the rules. Since these were going to be video depositions, Joel directed me on how to sit, where to look, and what to do with my hands. Do not pause for too long before you answer. Answer only the question asked. Never, ever swear. It went on and on. During a break I asked two young attorneys, both women, how much of my email they had to read. They reported they had read all of it. I have only one email account for both my work and personal life. "All of it? As in every email?" Indeed, every email for the last two years. "Including the ones from the guys about the trips to Mexico?"

"Yup." I began apologizing profusely. They started laughing at me and explained how bland the emails were. "They talk like boys talk when it is just boys talking." The lawyers did a lot of work with bankers, and apparently we did not come close to the usual standard for bad email behavior.

My training complete, it was time for the first deposition. Another long conference room table, this one downtown. There were fifteen lawyers sitting down the sides, with a video camera at one end and me at the other. The grilling by various lawyers lasted an hour and a half before the first break. In the bathroom, Joel said my answers were fantastic but that I kept scowling. He suggested I try to look like a kindly professor explaining an answer. At the next break, Joel coached me that my face was much better, but my answers were significantly worse, so I should go ahead and scowl. Unknown to me, I scowl when I am thinking hard.

By the second day of the first deposition, the DOJ refused to believe that I didn't carry a cell phone. They were sure I was talking to other publishers, and they thought I had a burner phone or a cutout. First, they suspected my wife was relaying messages, so they demanded access to her computer and phone. We agreed to produce both. Then they turned their focus to my thirteen-year-old son. Why did I use his phone when I was shoveling the road? Did he call people on my behalf? They demanded we produce his phone. Joel, perhaps even more pissed off than I was, told them they could have Jack's phone when a judge said so, and not before.

Many of the DOJ's questions seemed completely random to me. In the middle of a line of questioning, one of their lawyers asked me what game Eddy and I watched when Eddy came to my house. I said the Jets. He asked if the Jets had won or lost? I answered, with some confidence, that they had won. At the next break our lawyer asked me, "Are you sure the Jets won?"

I said, "It was more than two years ago, but I'm pretty sure they did."

He admonished, "Never guess when under oath." The Jets had won the week before, but that game they had lost. Paul Sleven, a long-suffering Jets fan, remembered. We had to formally correct my testimony. I struggled to see the point.

On a more relevant topic, I was asked if anyone had discussed other publishers with me in the period when the buy buttons were turned off. I replied, "Yes." They asked who, and I replied, "Sally Richardson of St. Martin's Press." They asked what she said, and I replied, "Where the fuck are those other guys?" I said it while looking at Joel, who almost spit up his coffee.

In a later deposition I was handed an Apple email to read, and I was asked a question about the first paragraph. I remained silent, my eye skimming down the page looking for context. And there toward the bottom was an email snippet from Steve Jobs, a clump of sentences about how well he thought I was handling the Amazon situation. I read the whole paragraph again word for word, grinning no doubt, in a silent room full of lawyers while the video cameras rolled.

As the depositions dragged on, there seemed to be ever more lawyers in the room. By the end, the Apple attorneys would show up to monitor progress. Sometimes there would be a nice spread during the lunch break, no doubt billed to one plaintiff or another. The conversations around the food were animated. In no case were the lawyers for other defendants allowed to talk to me, nor I to them; there could be no sharing of information. But there was one Apple attorney who enjoyed skirting the rules. He would stand far away from me, but then describe things to his colleagues in an extremely loud voice: "I just can't believe that meeting with Amazon staff that Bezos had in his boathouse was so innocent."

I was deposed five times, totaling thirty hours, spread out over two and a half years, all on video. Often the same questions were repeated, sometimes years apart. I answered every question carefully, trying to think of the questions that would follow depending on how I answered. The final deposition, taken almost five years after the events happened, lasted eight hours and was particularly grueling. At the end of the long day, as I was walking out through the cavernous lobby of the office building, I stopped, seemingly unable to move myself forward. It was an odd state of momentary suspension; I assumed the physical effect of mental exhaustion.

All the while there was ceaseless pressure to settle the case with the DOJ. Penguin settled, which left us as the only publisher who wouldn't. The intensity kept going up. The *Wall Street Journal* started researching my life for a profile that I tried to stop. It was going to be called "The Last Man Standing." Our general counsel, Paul Sleven, took a vacation to Barcelona and promptly had a heart attack on the plane. I told him a few days later that he was off the case, that it was not worth the risk to his health. He told me he felt that was his decision to make, not mine, and he would be back on the job shortly.

The judge in the case finally pushed us to mediation. The mediator would be a federal judge, Kimba Wood, who famously had to withdraw from an attorney general nomination over Nannygate.[9] We met in her chambers at the federal courthouse in lower Manhattan, and she brought all of us pastries for breakfast. It was a full day of lawyers arguing. The settlement, if we could reach one, would be for the DOJ, state, and class lawsuits, but the DOJ was in charge. We started together, all of us in one room debating the case. Then Judge Wood met separately with each side. Then all back together. The day dragged on in this fashion; Judge Wood was tireless and cheerful throughout.

During a break, when the judge was with the team of government lawyers, Joel took me to see the courtroom where the trial would take place. He pointed out the large video screen and explained they would have all my depositions tagged, and that if I answered the same question differently in court, they would play the tape. Questions like, "What did you discuss with Brian Napack at your lunch on December 14, 2009?"

At the end of the long day of mediation, Judge Wood called us in and gave me a message from the government of the United States. "They told me to ask if you fully realize they are capable of bankrupting your company."

I was completely speechless. Finally, I managed to ask, "Judge Wood, is that OK with you?"

She said, "No, no, that is not OK with me, but my only job is to give you the message."

---

9   In 1993, President Clinton nominated Zoe Baird to be his attorney general. The nomination failed because Zoe had paid her nanny in cash and hadn't paid the taxes. Kimba Wood was put forth as the next candidate. She had paid her nanny in cash, which was legal when she did it, and had paid the taxes as well, but politically it was too difficult. The two failed nominations became known as Nannygate.

The judge called the DOJ back in and asked them for their final settlement offer. They were smug when they told her how much they felt Macmillan should pay. She asked us for our proposed number. Ours was much lower, but still enormous. I tried not to show the bitterness I felt. Then Judge Wood looked at the DOJ guys sternly and said, "I'm going with his number," pointing at me. They protested, one of them loudly. They claimed it had to be a number in the middle. She gave them a hard stare, none of her previous charm on display, and repeated herself. "The number is his number."

I went back to the office and discussed settling with Paul. I was still reluctant; I knew we were not guilty. Finally, I suggested that in not settling I was probably being either stupid or stubborn. Paul replied, "Those are not mutually exclusive."

I called Eddy and asked if we would cause him problems if we stepped down, and he graciously said they would prefer to go it alone as it made the case simpler. The next day we folded our tents and wrote a huge check. For me, the settlement was humiliating in every respect. Apple fought on; they could afford what we could not, and I sensed they wanted to defend their old boss. Steve Jobs had died six months before the case began, and many at Apple still mourned. The cost of the case for us, from beginning to end, was close to $30 million.

In the trial between Apple and the DOJ, I was called as a hostile witness by the government. They allotted an afternoon and the following morning to grill me on the stand. On June 10, 2013, just before going into the courtroom, I met with Joel and asked if I could change tactics from all my depositions. I described what I intended, and he said it would be OK. I thought I detected a little smile. The courtroom was packed, and the seats on the side were full of lawyers, standing room only. There were seventeen lawyers officially involved on the record that day, never mind all their colleagues. The rows in the middle of the floor were full of reporters and people involved with the case, including my wife, and in the back, a pal and a few of my son's friends from school. It was a long walk down the aisle to my seat in the front, and as I walked in the place got quiet.

Judge Denise Cote did not like me much. She would occasionally glance down at me from her perch, all stony business. In court she referred to me, accurately, as being unrepentant. The questioning began, and instead of finding a way to honestly answer no, as I had in all my depositions, I tried to answer yes. On occasion, this led down a long line of questions that I answered with yes. Then when the DOJ lawyer asked his final triumphant question, I could answer no. It was a game of cat and mouse that caught the lawyer completely off guard. He became unsettled. The judge scowled at him repeatedly, and by the end of the afternoon his fists were clenched in exasperation. It made no difference in the outcome of the trial. It was a grueling day for him and for me. But it sure felt good whenever I gave my final one-word answer of "no" and his face would fall. At the end of my testimony, walking past the two-deep row of lawyers, I got handshakes, some big smiles, and from the Apple lawyer, a discreet high five.

On the way out of the building I ran into the government's lead investigation lawyer. We had always thought it ironic that his name was John Read. I liked the guy, but when he said he hoped we might work together again at some point, I told him it was nothing personal, but I hoped to never see him again for as long as I lived. We laughed, but my response wasn't entirely in jest.

The court found against Apple. Apple appealed, and we joined them in that appeal. I sat in on the 2nd Circuit Appellate trial, a guest, not a witness. It was clear from the questioning that two of the three judges would affirm. But it was a pleasure to watch Dennis Jacobs, the grizzled head justice, put the government through the wringer. He could not grasp how Amazon wasn't the antitrust problem in the case. He said things like "Drug dealing is the only case where new entrants to the market is a negative" and that publishers were "like mice getting together to put a bell on the cat." He, like Judge Wood before him, thought the government had it wrong from the beginning.

Apple lost in the 2nd Circuit, and then appealed the case to the Supreme Court. On March 7, 2016, the Supreme Court refused to hear Apple's appeal. That refusal triggered Apple's $400 million settlement payment and brought the eight and a half years of battle to a close.

It's hard to say who won in the end. Ebook consumers got a total of $566 million in rebates that went out in tiny checks over time. The DOJ, the states, and Canada all got settlements or won in court. The class action lawyers got a big piece of the pie; they made a ton of money for their meager effort. Amazon made money, but they lost on the pivotal point: they no longer controlled the price of ebooks—they couldn't discount. The publishers now controlled the price of ebooks, a great victory, but their pockets were a lot lighter. Physical booksellers won. Authors won, and Macmillan found ways to hold them harmless during the battle, which is how it should be. My hair got darker again, at least for a while, but I felt hollowed out. I had no sense of a victory.

In the fall of 2016, at a book fair in Frankfurt, Germany, Russ Grandinetti and I walked to the McDonald's in the train station for our traditional dinner. We talked about various issues, and toward the end of our meal I finally asked him the question that had been bothering me. "Russ, after all the testimony, all the discovery, and knowing me all these years, do you honestly believe I colluded back in 2009? I am talking about me specifically, not the others."

Russ, ever sharp, ever fast on his feet, replied, "I honestly believe that you believe you were innocent."

And that drew the matter to a close for me; his answer, in some ways, as unsatisfactory as the outcome of the lawsuit. And then, five years later, in an unlikely conversation with my daughter, my views of the outcome shifted.

Kyle teaches third grade in a low-income school district in Denver. Her class is always full of immigrant kids, and English is mostly a second language. In 2021, she had two kids from Afghanistan in her class, so when the Kabul airlift happened mid-year, they put all the new arrivals in her class as well. Three new kids. Two girls and a boy; the two girls could not read or write in any language. One day they all came to class with their interpreter and told Ms. O'Keefe they needed a place to pray once a day during school hours, as their faith required. They were distraught. Kyle promised she would find them a place. They became incredibly excited.

Kyle found a tiny room that was free. She booked it and told her administration what she planned to use the room for. Hours later, she was told that lawyers at the district level had decided it would not be allowed. Kyle was angry. She stormed home and spent Friday and Saturday researching the law. The law was clear. Schools have the obligation to provide children a place to pray, a legal standard set for fundamentalist Christians.

On Sunday Kyle called me. She said she had watched me fight these battles for years, and it always made her proud. Would I advise her on this one? We talked for an hour. Her plan was a good one; she intuitively knew the right steps. She had written a five-page paper presenting her arguments, including legal case references. I coached her a bit. She sent her paper Sunday night. On Monday the school relented.

The eight-year-old kids got their place to pray because their teacher fought for what was right. As a father, playing my small role, there could be nothing sweeter. It was years after the long ebook battles, but for me, there was a win in the end.

20.

Last Night I Dreamed

MATTHEW SHEAR SMILED A LOT. HE HAD AN EXPRESSIVE GAP-toothed grin, but it was more than that. When he smiled his whole face got in the act—even his eyes smiled. The smile was often joined by a quick rumbling laugh, lots of baritone with a touch of huskiness. And always loud, and I do mean loud. When I spoke at events, laboring with a less than perfect starting joke, I would hear his laugh booming from the back. And then the room would follow. No matter the size of the venue, you would hear that generous laugh.

Matthew was devoted to his job as the publisher of St. Martin's Press, and he worked tirelessly. He was remarkably creative and loved nothing more than a hokey marketing scheme. He was shameless in promoting books, happy to do whatever it took. When he was young, there was a famous photography book of shirtless male stars of the day called *Hunks*. Matthew published the parody book called *Chunks* and, being chunky, agreed to pose shirtless for the cover. In later years, Matthew would dress in a tutu or sing tasteless jingles, anything to sell a book.

Though he was the publisher, he did not directly manage lots of people at SMP. But most of the employees, particularly the young ones, felt he was somehow in their corner, using his power to help them. He knew how to get people to work together, and he never minded if he didn't get the credit.

One day I stopped by Matthew's office and noticed his face was ashen. I asked how he was. He said he was fine, just a little under the weather. I thought nothing of it. But over the next few months I noticed an occasional change in his skin color. One day I arrived at his office, and he looked gray. He said he was fine, but this time I wasn't buying it. Over the years we had been through some tough management moments together, and we had grown comfortable being direct. I closed his door, sat down, and told him I needed to know what was wrong.

The answer was worse than I had feared; it was advanced lung cancer. Matthew had been quietly taking Thursday afternoons off for chemo, working Fridays when the effects were minimal, and then dealing with the harsh realities of the chemo on the weekends. Monday morning, back to work as usual. He didn't want anyone to know, he was not interested in complaining, and he did not want sympathy. I thought he might want time off from work. He said he loved his job, and he wanted to be at his desk. And so, the months passed. There were rumors that occasionally floated up, Matthew seemed short of breath on the stairs or was a bit low on energy, but only a couple of people knew the truth.

For several years Matthew and his protégée, Jen Enderlin, had been pursuing Patricia Cornwell to come to SMP. Now, suddenly, there was an opportunity. Patricia was thinking of changing publishers, and she agreed to come by the office with her agent, Esther Newberg. Esther was an old friend of Matthew's, and he liked our chances. Jen and he worked up a presentation, and Matthew brought out the salesmanship that was his second nature. The meeting went well; Matthew was his old self, the energy pouring forth, the humor in flashes, the tone all business. I watched, an unnecessary third wheel. After the meeting Jen and Matthew went across the street for a drink to celebrate and compare notes; it was their standard practice after a big day. That night, Matthew went to the hospital for the last time.

I would go up and visit him. Sometimes he was all there, sometimes he was out of it, but he always seemed to enjoy having his feet rubbed, which became my task. Jen flew back from her vacation to sit with him. His family graciously allowed a few of us repeated access. Finally, he was allowed to go home. I visited him that night. He was in hospice care and was peaceful. He couldn't communicate but you got the sense he could hear. The family and their oldest friends had dinner in the next room, and I sat alone with Matthew for an hour. He fidgeted for a bit, so taking the cue, I rubbed his feet. We were silent but you could hear his family talking in the room next door, and you could feel the warmth. Then a smile came, but this time a small one. Matthew died early the next morning, just twenty-eight days after his remarkable last performance at work.

The company was distraught. People were crying at their desks, many of the young people experiencing their first great sense of loss. I was not much better.

That summer I decided that as a tribute to my old friend I would ride my bike from the plains to the top of the Bighorn Mountains in Wyoming. I would do it without stopping and with no pause in my thinking of him. I didn't make it, the road was too steep, the air too thin. The next summer I got in better shape and tried again. This time I reached the top. I got off the bike at Powder River Pass and climbed a high ridge. There was no trail; I scrambled over slopes of jumbled rock. The rocks here are among the oldest surface rocks on earth. Walking on three-billion-year-old granite is good fodder for thoughts of mortality. At the top of the third summit along the ridge I rested, had some final thoughts of Matthew, and turned to head home. As I walked down the west side of the ridge I came upon a small piece of flat land, an island of tundra in a great sea of old stone. It was roughly circular in shape, about ten feet across, and the grass was just turning brown. I stayed there a bit and built a stone monument that looked out over the snow-capped peaks to the north. It would be impossible to find again, but somewhere up on that ridge are Matthew's rocks, placed as best as I know how.

Two strange things happened in the years that followed. There is no way to explain them, and I don't try. About six months after Matthew died, I was in La Jolla, California, killing time, wandering the main drag. I saw an art gallery with a spectacular series of nature photographs. Curious, I went in. It was the usual fare of eagles, bears, and mountains, extremely well done. The owner said there were a few different pictures in the back by the same photographer. I walked around the corner and saw a single photograph on the wall facing me. It was a very large picture of the Flatiron building at late dusk. All the lights were off in the building except for one. The point office on the sixteenth floor. Matthew's office. And the photographer had enhanced the light coming from the window. It glowed.

A year or two went by. Jen and I would talk about Matthew on occasion. She, being the better person, kept in touch with his family. On an otherwise normal night, I had a remarkable dream. Matthew was there at my bedside. Unlike any other dream I have ever had, he seemed to actually be there. I didn't say anything, but he talked to me about how hard it was adjusting to being in a new place. I woke up with a clear memory of his voice, and it was his current voice, not something from the past. It rattled me a bit, so the next morning I went to see Jen. I told her I had a dream about Matthew. She interrupted me and said she had a dream about

Matthew. We compared notes in detail. It was the same dream. On the same night. She asked me if I knew what day it was. I had no clue.

It was Matthew's birthday.

21.

"Good"

JOCKO WILLINK AND LEIF BABIN WERE WEARING EXTREMELY tight suits. They were big, muscular men with buzz-cut hair and short necks. They talked loudly and bristled with physical authority. As military guys they looked out of place in a conference room full of publishing types. It clearly didn't bother them a bit.

They told us about the book they were writing called *Extreme Ownership*. It was about taking lessons from the battlefield and applying them to business. They illustrated each business point with a combat story from the war in Iraq. The stories they told were mostly from the battle for Ramadi, the most intense conflict of the war. It was the Navy SEALs in action, and it was hair-raising stuff. Jocko seemed to channel the intensity; you could feel the heat of it.

We left the meeting convinced that these guys would destroy anything that got in their way. We hoped by some twist of fate it wouldn't be us. We had already acquired the book, and only later discovered we had been the only publishers interested. They

205

finished polishing the manuscript, and we published it. The book got off to a fast start, mostly due to their charisma on television.

Leif's girlfriend, now his wife, worked as on-air talent for Fox News. The head of Fox News, Roger Ailes, offered to throw a party for the boys at the Waldorf Astoria, his guest list, our dime. It came together at the last minute. Our editor, Marc Resnick, called me a few days later. "Hey, you're going to the party tonight, right?" Damn. I wanted to go, I needed to go, but the way I was dressed wouldn't get me in the door. I ran over to a clothing store across the street and was unhappy to discover a limited supply of suit jackets. I surely wasn't going to buy a blazer. So, I grabbed a leather jacket-looking thing, passed on buying a tie, and headed back to the office. Then work got busy; I was running late. As I rushed to get out the door, I realized the jacket had two problems. First, it was made for winter, and it was a warm and muggy night in New York City. Second, it was unquestionably ugly. No wonder it was on sale.

Arriving at the Waldorf, I put on the jacket and went up to the ballroom. I was overheated. Sweating. The jacket weighed a ton and looked like crap. Someone said I better go see our cohost Roger, and they directed me to a crowded table where one guy was holding court. I went up and introduced myself, "Hi Roger, I'm John Sargent."

The guy started laughing, then waved across the table at an unassuming man who was looking at us. "I'm not Roger, that's Roger." Now it was not the heat that was making me uncomfortable. I chatted a bit with Roger, who was distracted and clearly not enjoying the small talk. The night was not going well.

I spied Jocko standing nearby and decided I might as well just keep trying. I walked up with a casual "Hi Jocko, I'm John Sargent."

He gave me a complete deadpan stare and said, "I know who you are." I told him how well I thought they were doing with the publicity, how well the book was selling, and asked him to keep up the good work. He responded, without a trace of a smile, "Yeah, sure. But I have a question for you. When are we going surfing?"

Where did that come from? I responded, "Well, I come to San Diego occasionally . . ."

Jocko stepped forward and put his finger on my chest. "Maybe you didn't hear me. I asked you, when are we going surfing?" That was one powerful finger.

"How about sometime next month?"

He replied, "Good." Leif was standing over on the side, and I saw him quietly smile, enjoying Jocko in action.

Later Jocko made a speech. He talked about those who didn't come home. In particular, he told us about a guy in his unit who jumped on a grenade so others could live. Some of those others were in the room. The deadpan was gone; now you could see the emotion carved on Jocko's face. The next day I confirmed a date with Jocko and bought a plane ticket to San Diego.

I started surfing at the age of forty-eight, and though I have a lot of enthusiasm and decent balance, I lack both athletic ability and skill. Oddly though, I have a board in San Diego. I bought it a few years back, on a California surf trip when I couldn't find a rental; it was the only nine-foot longboard in the shop at the time. It is an oddly shaped and ungainly thing with a sharp point. The front third is painted a garish pink. It is no mystery why it was the last longboard available for purchase,

The ugly board lives at a friend's house, and I arrived there in time for a late dinner. The alarm went off a few hours later. A bit groggy, I put on my wetsuit and drove off to meet Jocko at first light. We planned to surf in front of his house. Jocko is a Navy SEAL commander with a black belt in jiu jitsu. I am a bad surfer with a silly-looking board.

I parked and Jocko was standing on his deck, in his wetsuit. He pointed at the cliffs across the road and to the ocean beyond. "Let's go." The sky was starting to turn pink, and I could see the waves crashing on the rocks. Jocko nicely refrained from commenting on my board. His board was short, a serious piece of equipment dwarfed by the man who held it.

We walked to the edge of the rock; it was an eight-foot drop into the water. He looked out to sea, then turned his head to say, "Make sure to jump just as a wave arrives. There is a big set coming." And with that, he jumped in. He was right about the big set. The first wave crashed against the rock; Jocko was looking back over his shoulder as he paddled out. Well, shit. I didn't know what to do with my big clunky board when I jumped, and those rocks were looking volcanically jagged. On the other hand, there was clearly humiliation involved in just standing there.

I took the plunge and survived. We paddled out together in the early morning light; we were alone except for two kids off to the left. It was Jocko's son and one of his pals. It seemed they had been instructed not to steal any waves from Mr. Sargent.

Jocko explained the break. "There are rocks over there, get out of the wave before you reach them. The takeoff is here and slightly further north." I nodded, and then saw lumps on the horizon: here came the next set. Jocko was remarkable to watch. He was massive, but compact, like a large stone. His thin board sank below the surface under his weight. As the wave gathered under him, he thrashed the water, and it seemed to boil around him. He popped up, more aggressive than graceful, and his stance was all forward, all power. His face was fierce as he came screaming down the wave. He was scarier than a dorsal fin.

We floated together, waiting for the sets. We talked about the book, his ambitions, and surfing. I asked him if the local surfers were territorial in these parts. He pointed south. "The next break down is one of the worst in California. They don't wear leashes, and if you paddle out with a leash on there will be problems." I asked what sort of problems. "If you drop in on a guy and you are wearing a leash you better be ready for a fight." I noticed that Jocko was wearing a leash.

I asked, "Has that ever happened to you?"

He gave me the Jocko hard look. "No." Later he explained that leashes were "allowed" at this break because of the rocks. Rocks seemed a bit of an understatement given the cliff we jumped off.

We caught our last waves; the light of day had arrived. We paddled over to a small strip of sand and climbed up the cliff. The trail up was about a foot wide, slick with mud, and had a sheer twelve-foot drop. A last bit of adventure as my board caught the wind and my feet slipped near the edge.

Back in the office, Jocko's books just kept selling, and his podcast audience kept growing. A particular podcast was circulated around the office. It featured a basic premise—what doesn't kill you makes you stronger. But that simple message got the full Jocko treatment. During his days as a SEAL, when things went wrong, Jocko's response was short and simple: "Good." A mission gone bad, "Good." A leg injury on a night jump, "Good." Every hurdle placed in your way is an opportunity to get better. Slowly Jocko's "Good" became part of the language in the office among those who worked on his books. Missed your budget this month? "Good." The books arrived with a misprint? "Good." I realized it might all be a bit macho for New York publishing, but I enjoyed it.

That summer I was surfing out on Long Island. It was a beautiful day, and I had a normal sort of longboard, nothing pointed or pink. It was all very mellow, long rides on friendly waves. Smiles all around. At the end of a ride, some backwash hit my board, and my board hit my head. Hard. Putting my hand to my right ear, I discovered the ear lobe was hanging down, torn almost off. Immediately I thought: "Torn ear. Good." Such was the influence of Jocko Willink.

22.

Advice on Speaking in Public

Sharing

By all reports at SMP, Gerry Spence could be a difficult man.
He was the defense lawyer in the Karen Silkwood case. He had
defended the Weavers in the Ruby Ridge case. He generally fought
for the underdogs, and in his long career he had never lost a capital
case. He famously rejected an offer to be on the Dream Team for
the O. J. Simpson trial, then chose instead to be the nightly trial
commentator on CNN. Gerry is large. His huge head has both
piercing blue eyes and a flowing mane of white hair. He is rarely
seen in public without a fringed buckskin jacket. As a lawyer he
is famed for charming juries. As an author he fought endlessly for
better terms, not just for himself, but for all authors. His big book
was *How to Argue and Win Every Time*, and he seemed determined
to prove he could do that.

When I arrived at St. Martin's Press, he was one of the few big
names on our list. He had promised the sales force a trip to his

ranch if his book hit #1 on the bestseller list, and when it did, he made good on his word. But all that success did not stop him from causing agitation, so much agitation that I was called in to help. Before meeting with him, I discovered from the manuscript of his new book that we shared the same hometown. That would not be so odd if the town in question wasn't Sheridan, Wyoming, population 11,000. With that useful nugget of information, I called the man and introduced myself. He railed at me over a contract point or two, I brought up Sheridan, and that started a long friendship that would go way beyond work.

Some years ago, I was on the phone with Gerry about one of his books. At the end of the call, he asked how everything was going. I confessed that I was nervous about a speech I would be giving that coming weekend. I explained that it was an important moment, that I needed to win over the assembled audience. I needed to set a tone for the company. Most importantly, I needed to make sure the sales force left the room fully charged. I had decided to take a big risk in my speech, and there was a significant chance I would embarrass myself horribly.

Gerry's voice got paternal; clearly he felt it was a teaching moment. He told me that whenever things got tough in a case, and he was nervous before a jury, the first thing he did was tell them. He gave me this advice: "If you feel nervous, tell them you are nervous. And don't worry if your voice shows that to be true. If you are anxious, they will root for you to do well, and then you will have them."

I took his advice and added a paragraph to my speech. The next night, after giving the main body of my talk, I paused, then told the assembled employees and authors how much anxiety I had about what I was going to do next. I spoke of how I planned to reach beyond my abilities, and that I hoped for their support. Then I told them that I would end my speech with a history of the company, told entirely in rap. I let my nervousness show. People responded by expressing their enthusiasm for the endeavor. It was unaccompanied, the best I could manage, and bad by any measure. But people urged me on, they laughed, and at the end everyone jumped to their feet. Because Gerry was right.

Going Hungry

At around the same time, I sat at a lunch next to a famed PBS host. We were in Washington. The room was large and full, and there were notables dotted about the place. My PBS tablemate was an honoree at the grand event, but he was also introducing one of the notables. He was a pleasant guy, and we were happily chatting when the food arrived. As the talk turned to gossip, I noticed he wasn't eating his food. I asked him if he felt OK, or if he was nervous. No, he was fine, and this sort of speech was old hat. I finally just got to the point: "Why aren't you eating?"

"Oh," he replied, "I never eat before I speak." He seemed incredulous that anyone would eat before giving a speech.

Feeling ignorant, I asked, "Why is that?"

His answer was definitive. "If you eat, how can you be sure there isn't, say, a piece of spinach in your teeth?"

I still eat before I speak in public, call me a risk taker, but now I always run my tongue over my teeth before I start.

23.

Mandela and Morris

TERRY MORRIS AND I STARTED AT MACMILLAN AT ABOUT THE same time. She began as a rookie contracts administrator, working in our South African office in Johannesburg. She rose steadily through the ranks, all the way to the top. Over the years, we would see each other in the London office on rare occasion. When I took over responsibility for our South African company, I knew I should fly down to visit Terry. But it is a long flight, and a small company; the trip was easy to put off.

The compelling reason to go arrived in the summer of 2017 when we announced the publication of *Dare Not Linger*, Nelson Mandela's last book. The launch party in Johannesburg was planned for the night before the book went on sale in mid-October. It was decided that if the CEO from New York was going to show up in South Africa, that would be the time. I agreed to go, and Connie would join me. I assumed it would be the normal sort of company visit, a few words with the employees, a lunch or two, a review of the operation, and a pub party in a nice venue. Boy, was I ever wrong.

* * *

My visit started normally enough, a meeting in the office to discuss results and plans going forward. Then there was a staff meeting and speech in the break room, a small room that all the employees fit into comfortably. Folks were engaged; their questions were interesting, and different from what I was used to. After that it was off to a conference room to do the financial reports. Halfway through, Terry suddenly left the room. She came back twenty minutes later, and at the next break I asked her where she had gone. She responded that she'd needed to get out the payroll. Surprised, I asked, "You mean to tell me you do the payroll yourself?"

She looked at me quizzically. "Of course."

In the early afternoon, Terry took me to visit one of the city's best independent bookshops. As we approached the center of Joburg, she suggested nicely that I roll up my window. It was a lovely day, so I asked why. She pointed a few blocks ahead to a traffic light and said, "If we stop at that light with the windows down, someone is likely to reach into the car and take anything they see of value." There was no judgment in her voice, just stating the facts. I rolled up my window.

We parked on a bustling street. Terry hopped out, and we walked around the corner, through a doorway, and into an internal courtyard. We climbed some exposed stairs to the mezzanine level. One half of the mezzanine was the bookshop. Terry hugged the owner like a long-lost brother, and while they chatted, I wandered the shelves. It was a small, narrow space, dusty from exposure to the street. The books were spine out and mostly used. I could not understand how this could be a business. Later Terry explained that very little was sold inside the store. In the mornings the staff would gather, load up with books, and take them to numerous informal traders. The traders would then set up card tables on the streets to sell the books.

We went back to the office in time to get ready for the publication party at the Nelson Mandela Foundation. I went early, catching a ride with some people from work. It was a lively trip; our little group was in high spirits. When we arrived, I was whisked away for a tour of the archives. We went down into the basement. There were several large low-ceilinged rooms, kept cold and dry, full of extraordinary history. The personal curator of Nelson Mandela's effects showed me things as we wandered through: important writings in Mandela's own hand, keepsakes, historical documents. And, sitting randomly on top of a file cabinet, the gifts brought to him by the Obamas.

The time came for the start of the event, and I was shepherded upstairs and into a side room. Connie and Terry arrived, and by the time we entered the main room it was already completely full, probably three hundred people in their best finery, modern, traditional, and everything in between. Drinks were served, and the enthusiastic crowd was directed into a lecture hall with stadium seating, standing room full. As I walked in the door, I was startled to see banks of lights and numerous TV cameras. It was clear that the event would be broadcast live, and I saw with some alarm that the two seats in the middle of the front row had cards on them that said Sargent. Terry confirmed that the event would be televised nationally on the networks and went to prepare for her speech.

I sat next to a fantastic older guy, and we started talking. He was cheerful and funny, and the conversation was easy. After the speeches started, we whispered the occasional aside. I discovered later that he was Chief Buthelezi, a leader in one of the opposition parties who had spent time in the ANC with his old friend Nelson Mandela. The crowd was full of family members, leaders of the ANC, and dignitaries. People spoke of their time in prison with the great man and the struggle they faced together after prison. Then Terry stepped up to the mic and delivered a flawless speech about the book and its cultural importance. Feeling full of pride, I sat up straight with my hands in my lap, trying to look dignified for the cameras.

The next day we flew to Cape Town, and the airport bookstores had stacks of the book on display. The front page of every newspaper had pictures of the event and the book. It struck me then just how much impact Terry and her small staff had on the attention of a nation. And just how remarkable it was that a single man, Nelson Mandela, could mean so much to the world.

24.

Hello and Goodbye

NEW YORK PUBLISHING IS FULLY STOCKED WITH DEMOCRATS, mostly left of center. When the word got out that both Michelle and Barack Obama would be writing books, you could feel the frenzy mount. There was auction fever before the auction was announced.

Bob Barnett, a lawyer who had worked for presidents and other politicians for decades, would be selling the books. Bob finally announced the auction and told publishers how it would work. During the first week, we would be invited to Washington to meet with Michelle. During the second week, we would go to the same location and meet with the president. There would be two separate auctions for the books, also one week apart. This news became the only conversation in publishing; the industry was vibrating.

We met with Michelle at the new Obama Foundation offices. The Obamas were just moving in, so much so that Michelle had not yet seen the artwork at the front desk. She later reported this to us sheepishly, explaining that for security reasons they had not walked through a front door in eight years.

Michelle arrived at the same time we did; there was a commotion at the door of a small conference room. Hellos were exchanged all around. "Hi. I'm Michelle." It was all very casual. She had not decided what exactly she wanted to write, but she knew the purpose was "building a strong woman from a small girl." The conversation was full of give and take about what the book might be. At the end, she stood at the door as we filed out. She seemed genuinely thankful for the meeting. I was the last guy in line and was expecting the usual receiving line handshake. Instead, I got a big thank you, a bigger smile, and a robust hug. For the record, she was wearing a Diane von Furstenberg wrap dress. I knew what question I would be asked when I got home.

The next week it was back to the same airport gate. It was the same plane ride and the same cab trip to the Foundation. We were ushered into the same conference room. But this time seats were assigned, and we waited with the door closed. I was seated in the chair opposite the door, with a vacant chair at the head of the table on my left. There was no banter; it was clear this would be a different sort of meeting. Then there was a sudden burst of activity, and in strode the president. We all rose to our feet. He worked his way around the table, stopping to greet the four of us individually. The person on my right walked toward him and said a few words. That left a sizable gap between the president and me. His focus shifted my way. Clearly, he had been briefed—he knew what roles we all played. He walked toward me with a smile and stuck his hand out.

But here is the thing. Instead of sticking his hand straight out, he stuck it out with his arm angled to the right. My response was instinctual from my younger days; I stuck my hand out with my arm farther to the right than his. He adjusted his arm outward again as he strode forward; we slapped our hands together. I had planned on a normal shake and "Good to meet you, Mr. President." What came out of my mouth was "Hey, man."

At that he gave me a bemused smile and a single arched eyebrow. He said something like, "Nice to meet you, John." He sat down and so did I. My mind focused on a simple question: *Did I really just greet the president of the United States of America by saying "Hey, man"?* How could that possibly be?

The meeting was lively from the start. John Sterling of Henry Holt was sitting across the table from me; he would be the editor of the book if we got it. John is an old-school Yankee with this incredibly thick hair. He is a tall man, and the hair stands high. Early in the meeting John asked a pointed question. In answering the question, Bob Barnett made a reference to John's hair. John was immediately defensive, until the president raised his hand to stop him from talking. In the following silence, the president looked him in the eye and said, "John, when you have hair like that, you've got to own it."

The conversation continued and the president, with pride, discussed the competence of his administration. He used the Gulf oil spill as an example. After telling us how they figured out how to cap the well—apparently a solution drawn on a napkin—one of his aides goaded him: "And then there was the pelican."

Suddenly we saw some Obama passion. "Man, I hated that pelican." He carried on, "Every day we would do these fantastic new things to close down that well, the results were remarkable. And every night on the news they would just show the images of that goddamn pelican, covered with oil." The pelican came up again later, and again with the passionate presidential modifier, goddamn.

When it came time to leave, the president stood at the door as we filed out. I was again last in line, and we chatted for a minute. As I left, he stuck his hand straight out and so did I. It was a business shake, and I looked him straight in the eye and said, "It was great to meet you, Mr. President." He gave me an upturned lip corner, and with a twinkle in his eye responded, "And it was nice to meet you, John."

Random House won both of the Obama books. I am pretty sure it was about the $65 million they reportedly offered, not my "Hey, man" greeting.

25.

Fire and Fury

S TEVE RUBIN, THE PRESIDENT OF HENRY HOLT, WAS ALREADY
breathless. "Meet me in Don's office, you are not going to
believe this." When I arrived, Steve and Don Weisberg, his boss,
were on Don's big leather couch. I took a chair and Steve, without
preamble, launched into his report. "I just got off the phone with
Michael. He told me he had good news and bad news. The good
news was that President Trump woke Michael up last night and
ranted in his ear for a half hour. Michael couldn't get a word in
edgewise. Trump raged about anything and everything, and nothing he said was appropriate to share with a journalist." Don asked
about Michael's bad news, and Steve replied, "This country is in a
whole lot of trouble."

A few months before, shortly after Donald Trump was elected
president, Michael Wolff had called Steve. Michael claimed he
could get unfettered access to the West Wing to report on the
first one hundred days of the Trump presidency. He asked Steve
to allow him to set aside his current Holt project and to give him

a contract for a book about the inner workings of the new administration instead. We gulped at the price his agent suggested. We worried about how much access he would get, we worried about legal problems, and we worried about how long it would take to write the book. We worried about everything, but we concluded it was worth the risk. Michael put the plan in motion.

He began work immediately, and shortly after the inauguration, he started spending lots of time in the West Wing. The new administration was disorganized, and they quickly lost track of Michael. No one seemed to know who had approved his access, and no one seemed inclined to ask. The infighting was intense, and it was not clear to anyone which side had given Michael his seat at the party. We repeatedly asked Michael if he had to sign any documents limiting what he could do or say. As the weeks went by, we were surprised that he could continue to answer "no." The man was roaming freely in the halls, asking anyone and everyone questions, and he had a tape recorder. Over time he was given a place to sit, and the various warring factions in the White House would all gripe to him about each other.

At work, the sessions in Don's office continued. Steve would always begin the same way: "You are not going to believe this." The stories were appalling, startling, extraordinary. Some made it into the book. Some didn't.

There is a tradition of reporting on the first one hundred days of a presidency, and we were anxious to get the book out. But the administration didn't seem to realize they had agreed to a hundred days, and Michael was now in the West Wing continuously, a fixture more than a reporter. The Trump presidency was endlessly fascinating; the Russia investigation was in full swing. Charlottesville happened on day ninety-nine. We finally agreed that Michael would stay in place, and we quietly slipped the book, still unknown to most, into early 2018.

On August 18, 2017, President Trump fired Steve Bannon, his chief strategist and, unknown to almost everyone, the guy who had given Michael access. We all agreed that the president firing the man most responsible for getting him the job would be a good way to end the book. Michael left the West Wing as quietly as he had come. Over the next few months, he wrote ceaselessly, crafting two hundred days of chaos into a book.

As Michael wrote, Macmillan lawyers and external lawyers carefully read every word. We were not worried about President Trump. The president of the United States controls the world's largest bully pulpit, and the press is allowed to say what they please about him or her. But there were lots of other characters in this story, and the book had to be accurate to be credible.

When Michael finished the manuscript, we put him through days of legal review. He had a surprising number of his sources on tape, and as the meetings wore on, we became confident that even the most outlandish stories were either factual or were being reported as rumors. We asked Michael to drop several stories that did not have enough sourcing or were factually questionable.[10]

The lawyers signed off. Cloaked in secrecy, *Fire and Fury*, its title taken from a presidential tweet about North Korea, went to press. We placed it under embargo; no one was allowed to read it. Indeed, no one was allowed to see it. Booksellers were skeptical. We twisted every arm we could and managed to ship a relatively modest 90,000 copies.

We arranged for the *Washington Post* to run a story on January 6, the weekend before the book published. The *Today Show* would run two segments with Michael on Monday, January 8, and *New York* magazine would run an excerpt of the book on the pub date,

---

10 After the book came out, many of the people mentioned threatened to sue us, but in the end, nobody did. The truth is the best defense against libel claims.

January 9, 2018. The books would go on sale at the stroke of midnight. None of that happened.

* * *

On January 2, *The Guardian* got a copy of the book and reported on some of the content. The press embargo was broken; *New York* magazine followed with their excerpts and the *Washington Post* with their story. Sara Huckabee Sanders trashed the book in her White House press briefing. To our great surprise, the White House released an official statement; we had been hoping for a tweet or two. The *New York Times*, CNN, and the *Washington Post* broke the embargo, and then everyone followed. The book went from #40,000 on Amazon to #1. At Henry Holt, we received forty-five press calls in less than an hour. The messenger delivering a copy of the book to the Associated Press got lost and was physically chased down on the street by an AP staffer. We began negotiations with NBC for the first interview with Michael Wolff. All of this happened in four hours.

I had to give a speech the next day at our higher education sales meeting, so while everyone scrambled to react to the frenzy, I caught a flight to Arizona. Early the next morning I was alone in the gym on an elliptical trainer, earbuds in, music cranked up, the desert dark outside the windows. Someone came in and turned on the video screens that were scattered around the place, all on different channels. On every screen, there was Michael, or failing that, the book jacket. For two minutes my head was on a swivel; *Fire and Fury* was clearly the lead story on every channel. I needed a phone, and I needed one quick. I jogged back to room 6503, sat at the desk, and dialed work. One after another my calls went unanswered. Finally, after dialing executives at random, I reached someone who cheerfully reported that everyone was in Don's office, and would I like to interrupt them? I suggested that might be a good idea, and I was transferred into the meeting. Don asked if I was sitting down. Yes, I was. He reported that Donald J. Trump, the president of the United States, had just delivered a cease-and-desist letter to Michael Wolff and Henry Holt. I admit my first thought was an elated *Holy shit, we are gonna sell a ton of books*. Then I realized this went far beyond selling books, and my elation waned. A sitting president was attempting to subvert the First Amendment, and freedom of the press was usually the first freedom suspended by authoritarian regimes. The cease-and-desist was no small thing.

Trump's Hollywood lawyer, Charles Harder, promptly leaked the cease-and-desist letter to the press. The phones lit up. We immediately started work on a short statement saying we would go forward with the publication. Now we had to decide if we should hold the books until Tuesday as scheduled or move up the publication date. At this point we were already shipping books to stores; some booksellers would have them, and some wouldn't. The decision to move a publishing date forward is highly complex; it gives some accounts an advantage and it pisses everyone else off. And it is hard to stop those who do have the book from selling it. Most importantly, we knew we would send a message if we moved the pub date forward. Still in Arizona, I took the easy way out and left the decision to Don, whom I trusted completely. Don made a bold choice. On Thursday morning we announced in response to the president's letter that we would move the release date up to the next day, Friday. Every account was called, more books were ordered, shipping companies were pushed, media outlets were informed, and publicity schedules were adjusted. All hands on deck. A prominent blogger posted that moving the publishing date forward was, in effect, giving the middle finger to the president.

The phones in the sales department were ringing off the hook. Every account wanted more books, lots and lots more. There was not enough capacity at the printers, nor paper at the mills. There was a shortage of truck drivers. There was a bomb cyclone on the East Coast that closed the UPS hub in Toronto. Who had even heard of a bomb cyclone?

At my talk in Phoenix, I asked the gathered employees and authors if they wanted to hear my speech, or would they prefer to hear what it was like to be me on that particular morning. The one-sided response made it clear that everyone had already heard the news. I stayed for an hour, mostly answering questions, before hurrying back to room 6503 and the phone.

I got late checkout.

The greatest concern was getting books. We dealt with three big printers and two paper suppliers at the time. I wrote to the five CEOs and explained that we could not run out of this book now, not when the president was trying to suppress it. I asked them to work together, instead of competing, to quickly get us as many books as possible. The response was immediate and gratifying. Richard Garneau, the owner of Resolute Paper, a Canadian company and our largest paper supplier, wrote a note to all his plant managers: "You guys get Macmillan all the paper they need: where and when they need it. No excuses, make it happen." It didn't hurt that the president had recently started talking about tariffs on Canadian paper.

Trump's cease-and-desist letter demanded a response by Friday, and our lawyers were hard at work with outside counsel to get that done. I intervened and suggested that we break with standard protocol, ignore their timing request, and hold our answer until Monday. We would have one shot at this; we should make the most of it. To that end, I called Chris Finan at the National Coalition Against Censorship. I would be writing our public response, and my knowledge of First Amendment legal cases was limited. I asked Chris, a First Amendment scholar, for all the relevant Supreme Court decisions, and in particular the relevant language in the majority opinions. The justices are generally eloquent, and I hoped to use their words. Chris committed to getting me results in a day, and he and his staff got to work. I flew home, spending my entire time in the airport walking, a phone stuck to my ear.

The next morning Michael went on the *Today Show*. The book went on sale and promptly sold out everywhere. The president, aiding our cause, started tweeting. That afternoon, Chris, true to his word, delivered a stack of Supreme Court decisions. Across Macmillan, people focused on the complex logistics needed to get books delivered and more books printed. We dropped the special effects on the cover, changed the board material, and swapped out the hard-to-get paper. We used extra printers, including a printer in Germany to print the English language export edition for Europe.

On Friday night I sat down and thought about what we should do on Monday. I knew our outside lawyer, Elizabeth McNamara, was working on an extremely aggressive legal response. But I also knew we had to get out an explanation of what the president was trying to do and how very wrong it was. It would be difficult to address in a press release. I also knew that many of the people in our company did not fully understand the complexities of libel, the First Amendment, and how they fit together. It dawned on me that I could write a letter to our employees and release it to the press. Two birds, one stone.

I worked at home most of Saturday on a short note. Various people at Macmillan helped. The most difficult thing to convey was that Trump's letter wasn't a court filing or a lawsuit, and thus wasn't under court jurisdiction. Paul Sleven, our general counsel, finally figured out the right language: "We will not allow any president to achieve through intimidation what our Constitution precludes him from achieving in court." I added "or her" after "him." I finished the letter just after 5:00. I was particularly proud of the last line: "Mr. President, go fish." I thought it perfect, capturing the very essence of the matter. Connie pointed out that it might be more sophomoric than brilliant. I reluctantly changed it, and the last line is better for Connie's intervention.

Message from John Sargent: Fire and Fury

Last Thursday, shortly after 7:00 a.m., we received a demand from the President of the United States to "immediately cease and desist from any further publication, release or dissemination" of Michael Wolff's Fire and Fury. *On Thursday afternoon we responded with a short statement saying we would publish the book, and we moved the pub date forward to the next day. Later today, we will send our legal response to President Trump.*

Our response is firm, as it has to be. I am writing you today to explain why this is a matter of great importance. It is about much more than Fire and Fury.

The president is free to call news "fake" and to blast the media. That goes against convention, but it is not unconstitutional. But a demand to cease and desist publication—a clear effort by the president of the United States to intimidate a publisher into halting publication of an important book on the workings of the government—is an attempt to achieve what is called prior restraint. That is something no American court would order as it is flagrantly unconstitutional.

This is very clearly defined in Supreme Court law, most prominently in the Pentagon Papers case. As Justice Hugo Black explained in his concurrence:

Both the history and language of the First Amendment support the view that the press must be left free to publish news, whatever the source, without censorship, injunctions, or prior restraints. In the First Amendment, the Founding Fathers gave the free press the protection it must have to fulfill its essential role in our democracy. The press was to serve the governed, not the governors. The Government's power to censor the press was abolished so that the press would remain forever free to censure the Government.

Then there is Justice William Brennan's opinion in The New York Times Co. v. Sullivan:

Thus we consider this case against the background of a profound national commitment to the principle that debate on public issues should be uninhibited, robust and wide open, and that it may well include vehement, caustic, and sometimes unpleasantly sharp attacks on government and public officials.

And finally Chief Justice Warren Burger in another landmark case:

The thread running through all these cases is that prior restraints on speech and publication are the most serious and least tolerable infringement on First Amendment rights.

There is no ambiguity here. This is an underlying principle of our democracy. We cannot stand silent. We will not allow any president to achieve by intimidation what our Constitution precludes him or her from achieving in court. We need to respond strongly for Michael Wolff and his book, but also for all authors and all their books, now and in the future. And as citizens we must demand that President Trump understand and abide by the First Amendment of our Constitution.

—John

While we were working on the note, the president spent the day tweeting. Speaking of himself, he claimed, "the two greatest assets have been mental stability and being, like, really smart." He went on to define himself as "a very stable genius."

Sunday seemed calm, but unnoticed by any of us at the time, WikiLeaks posted the full text of *Fire and Fury*. They had found an unprotected PDF of the book that had been accidentally sent in an email by the British publisher. Over the next week WikiLeaks would push out free copies with a marketing campaign.

Monday arrived; it was time to respond to the president. We sent out the letter to our employees, and then leaked it to the press. I lost control of my inbox. Our outside attorney sent President Trump's lawyer our legal response. At the beginning she said, "As a result, you demand that my clients cease publication of the book and 'issue a full and complete retraction and apology.' My clients do not intend to cease publication, no such retraction will occur, and no apology is warranted." And at the end she said, "Lastly, the majority of your letter—indeed seven full pages—is devoted to instructing Henry Holt and Mr. Wolff in meticulous detail about their obligation to preserve documents . . . At the same time we must remind you that President Trump, in his personal and governmental capacity, must comply with the same legal obligations regarding himself, his family members, their businesses, the Trump campaign, and his adminis- tration, and must ensure all appropriate measures to preserve such documents are in place. This would include any and all documents pertaining to any of the matters on which the book reports."

If nothing else, we were direct. The press coverage was enor- mous and global. The International Publishers Association issued a statement of support for Macmillan. That night the book reached its peak rate of sale, 23,000 copies per hour at Amazon alone. My boss called from a conference in Europe; he was delighted, everyone there was reading the book. But he reported that they were reading it on their devices, for free. The WikiLeaks post was becoming a serious problem.

I had spent years helping negotiate an industry agreement with the guys at Google, and we had become friendly. I called them now and asked for their help. They agreed to make the takedown of the illegal edition of *Fire and Fury* their top priority globally. At Macmillan, we assigned two people to scan the web on a contin- uous basis looking for infringing copies. Normally it takes several days to take down a copyright violation, but Google was now get- ting it done in seconds.

By Tuesday, the original publication date for *Fire and Fury*, we had ordered 1.5 million books in twenty-two printings at five different printers, including the one in Germany. All of the books would be delivered within a week. For the German-language edition, we had hired seven translators to get the book out as quickly as possible. In the short gap before the German-language edition became available, the English-language version was the #1 selling book in Germany.

Fire and Fury, and Michael, dominated the news cycle for several weeks. A cultural moment is hard to define, but a *Saturday Night Live* opening skit is a good marker. It almost never happens for a book, but with Bill Murray playing Steve Bannon, it happened for this one.

Several weeks later, I gave my annual year-end speech to all our New York employees. I talked about the book and what it meant, to me and to our company. I asked Steve Rubin, who bought the book and published it, to stand up. There were cheers, of course. Then I asked John Sterling, the editor of the book, to stand. And then Maggie Richards and Pat Eiseman, who handled the marketing and publicity. Then I asked everyone at Henry Holt who worked on the book in any way to stand. Then everyone involved with the supply chain and printing the book, stand up. Alison Lazarus, our head of sales, and everyone who sold books to our accounts, stand up. By then there were more than six hundred people on their feet. I talked about the warehouse in Virginia that carried the load and our cousins in Germany. I called out twenty-six people throughout the company by name, ending with Don, who had tirelessly guided our efforts from beginning to end. And then I asked everyone who had told people about the book, and thus spread the word, to stand. Some folks may have still been in their seats at that point, but I couldn't see them. I asked everyone to give themselves a big hand. They all deserved the standing ovation.

26.

I'm as Good Once as I Ever Was

ARCH 2018, TWO MONTHS AFTER ALL THE FIRE AND FURY. There were nine of us at Stewpot Slim's, the small log cabin that passes for mid-mountain at the June Lake ski resort. Stewpot had closed up shop, but not before Jack, his ski buddies, and Connie had secured a fresh beer. We were soaking in the sun, our boots were loosened, our jackets were off, and Sirius Classic Rock was on the outdoor stereo. The late afternoon light had arrived. The young sat, chattered, and sang along to lyrics made popular before they were born.

We had arrived at this end-of-the-road ski hill that morning to find an empty parking lot. We piled out of the pickup, Connie and I from up front, and Jack from behind me, the same spot he has ridden in since his car seat twenty-three years ago. The hill had also been empty that day; we saw few people and six of them turned out to be Jack's ski-addicted pals. We had skied fast; the snow was hard packed, smooth and even. Connie declared it was her best day of skiing ever, and Jack clearly delighted in combining his friends with his mom and dad.

And so we were at Stewpot's, the day was done, just a short trip down to the parking lot left. I looked up and realized there was nobody on the slopes. Nobody. And there was no one on the chairlift. It occurred to me suddenly and with some force: here was a chance that would never come again.

I jumped up, grabbed my jacket and helmet, and clicked into my skis. Jack's friend Greg asked if I was going up. I replied in the affirmative. He said, "If you ski it really fast, and bear left halfway down, you can use the lift towers as gates, just one turn between each."

I heard myself respond, "Who said anything about turns?"

As I skied away, I heard him ask Jack, "Yo, is he serious?"

I was completely alone on the lift ride up. The craggy peaks and sheer faces of the Eastern Sierra cast shadows across the snow on their shoulders. The sun's angle deepened the furrows in the bark of the old growth ponderosa pines. The air was still, the sky a high-altitude blue. The silence of the mountains.

The clock at the top of the lift said 10:30, the same time it showed that morning. None of the clocks at June Lake show the actual time. I slid off the lift and took a moment at the top. The peaks stretched for miles, and Mono Lake shimmered in the distance. The sun was still warm on my back. I stuck my skis over the edge and looked down at Stewpot's cabin, a postage stamp, the scale too small to see the people. The slope was empty, with not a ripple in the snow. It was time to go.

I pushed over the edge and dropped straight down. I angled to the left, and now the first change of direction. Upper body forward, weight transfer, roll onto the uphill edge of the left ski. The edge tracked. Now release the skis early, angle downhill, and to the right. The snow was very fast, the rate of acceleration remarkable.

Now shift the weight again, still driving downward and bearing left. The edge held again. I was already carrying too much speed, but it would be straight downhill now. The wind became a physical force against my chest, stretching my clothes against me, loud in my ears. My skis were flat on the snow, and they began to wobble and slide underfoot. They were not made for this. I corrected course slightly to get on the ski's edges and they held. The slope eased slightly and there was only one way to go faster. I dropped into a tuck, chest on my knees; the right knee gave me a stab of pain. The skis were flat on the snow again and sliding all over the place. I had reached the top possible speed for this skier, on these skis, on this day.

Suddenly the slope went flat and the base of the chairlift flashed by. I stood from my tuck and dug in the edges. Ahead the entire population of Stewpot's was lined up on the front of the deck. There were yells and whoops. There were fist pumps and high fives. Greg told Jack later, "Bro, your dad is a fucking legend. He straight-lined chair 7!"

I am still fast.

27.

The Original Screen Man

EDWARD SNOWDEN IS A POLARIZING FIGURE. HE SAYS THAT A third of Americans love him, a third don't care about him, and a third hate him, hate him like he should be dead or in jail. In Germany, he is one of the most respected figures of his time. I had always been torn on the subject: a traitor, yes, but maybe justifiably.

When Ed decided to write a book, his agent approached just two editors, people he knew well and trusted completely. One of them worked at Macmillan. Our global bid for his book won the day, in part because we were fast. There was a lot of complexity to the deal; we would use a shadow company in Germany to pay him. No one could know that the book was coming, and Ed was understandably obsessed with security. He knew, and we knew, that the government would stop the publication of the book if they could.

There was a lot to coordinate. We would publish simultaneously in six countries and two languages, English and German. We needed to sell the rights in other countries and get the manuscript translated into their languages. All of this had to be done through secure channels without word of the book leaking. We planned to publish the book just twenty-eight days after announcing it. Ed was always working in the background, but a time came when I needed to talk with him directly. His agent, Christopher Parris-Lamb, had an encrypted computer with a secure link to Ed in Moscow. I traveled uptown to the Gernert Agency where Chris worked. It is a small office, and the owner of the agency is an old friend. I was hanging out in reception when Chris waved at me from down the hall. I walked into Chris's office. There was a computer on the desk facing the door, and a single chair facing the screen. And there on the screen was the famous face, Edward Snowden. "Hi, John," he said with a big smile.

"Hi, Ed." We talked about the book and how to market it. Ed is wicked smart.

The book came in, and it was beyond what we had imagined. After reading it I felt that Ed had tremendous courage, and like him or not, he had done what he did for the love of his country. He knowingly gave up his American life because in his mind it was the right thing to do. Even if you don't agree with his judgment, it was heroic. It was a story he had earned the right to tell, and we would help him tell it, even if it would make us unpopular with the government and a third of the country. Ed also had another purpose for writing the book. In telling his story he planned to tell people that they need to care about digital privacy, even if it wasn't important to them personally. He got that right.

As the project moved forward, we installed Ed's encryption software on a computer in a little conference room by my office. When his editor or the publicity people needed to talk to him, they had to use that computer. On occasion I would walk out of my office and oh, there was Ed on the screen. I would go in, stick my head in front of the camera, and say hi. He would greet me in return, we would wave, and I would go on with my day. It was deeply surreal every time.

In one of our screen conversations, Ed said that he always wore the same jacket in front of the camera. The next day Rodrigo, who designed the book jacket, and I went to a men's store across the street and bought him a new one. We had to guess the size. With the help of Ben, his lawyer at the ACLU, we got his mother to take it to him on her next visit to Moscow. It was like that, trying to find a way to connect, with obstacles at every turn.

The book came out, a modest success in the United States, but a monster hit in Germany. Ed did interviews around the world, always on a screen. The government came after us to stop any flow of funds to him, but that horse had left the barn.

Ed is complex, and at times he can be difficult. But he is living a life that is hard to imagine. He is always chased, always under surveillance and suspicion. He lives in isolation in Moscow, as far from home as he could be. Over the course of a year, I sent Ed lots of email, but always through Ben or Chris for encryption. We never talked on the phone. Ed and I would only see each other on the screen. Looking back, I realize I never saw more of Edward Snowden than his head and shoulders. I don't really know what the whole Ed looks like. He lives for most people not as a flesh and blood human or a voice, but as a face on a screen. Ed lives on Zoom, and he lived there before anyone else.

28.

This Is Your Song

IN LATE 2018 I GOT A CLANDESTINE EMAIL FROM THE EXECUTIVE board of Pan Macmillan in Australia. Ross Gibb, their boss, was about to have his thirtieth anniversary at the company. Could I possibly fly down to present him with his award? Of course I could. Ross had been running our Australian operation for over twenty-five years, and his Australian authored list was the best in the country. He is relentlessly competitive, a hearty soul in a compact body. We were kindred spirits from the beginning.

The thirtieth anniversary celebration was to be a surprise, and the planning needed to start immediately. The first decision was the code name, and after some debate we settled on Operation Salt (Ross's wife's name is Pepper). Operation Salt swung into gear. The anniversary event would take place during a sales conference at a small hotel an hour and a half outside of Sydney. It was decided that I should land in the morning and spend the day in Sydney; I might be seen if I came straight to the hotel. In the late afternoon, a car driven by a man named Michael would pick me up and drive me to the little town where the event was being held. We would drive around unseen until everyone had gathered at the appointed hour. Then Michael would be called, we would pull up in the restaurant parking lot, and I would be handed a cell phone. Ross would think I was calling from New York.

Remarkably, all went according to plan. As we pulled into the parking lot, Tracey Cheetham, the executive in charge of the event, flagged us down and handed me a phone. Ross came on the line, and I told him I was just calling to wish him a happy anniversary. As I talked, I walked into the room where the company was gathered. Ross was in the far corner with everyone packed around him; he didn't see me until I pushed through the crowd. His first laughing words were, "I knew you were here." It is hard to sneak anything by Ross. On the other hand, he is good at bluffing.

After dinner there was an anniversary party with speeches. Ross was forced to wear a crown and carry a scepter throughout the proceedings. He didn't seem to mind. The party was a rowdy event, full of shouts and free-flowing spirits. It did not go late though; everyone knew it was just the warmup. The next evening was the main event, the traditional costume party on the last night of the conference. The theme for the costumes traditionally came from a new book on the next season's list. The book this year was Elton John's autobiography. Australians love costume parties. You can imagine the excitement.

The sales meetings ended in the late afternoon, and the sleepy little hotel fell quiet. It takes time to dress up. The dinner itself was not remarkable. The food was average fare. The room was standard, a big square with medium height ceilings, round tables, and thinning carpet. There was a DJ setup and a dance floor at the far end. The decorations were simple, Elton John album covers hanging from the ceiling over the tables. There were about eighty people in attendance, almost all the employees of Pan Mac Australia and New Zealand. But this was no normal event.

Unbelievably, every single person at the gathering was in costume. Some people took the easy way out: a pair of big glasses, a hat, bright clothes, and a feather boa or two for good measure. Some went full Elton, outrageous outfits and massive flamboyant headgear. And some dressed as the songs. Praveen Naidoo, who would eventually run the company, wrapped his torso in black corrugated paper. On his head there was a vertical twist of orange cellophane, bent to the left at the top. He was a candle in the wind. Two slight young women in tutus held a massive, corrugated hand. Hold me closer, tiny dancer.

Dinner was raucous, a boisterous outpouring of enthusiasm. After dessert was served, the DJ spun the first song. As if on cue, all the women—and the company is mostly women—stood up and went to the dance floor. The male stragglers sat scattered among the tables. In a matter of seconds, the dance floor was packed. They were letting loose, hands waving. "Fame . . . I want to live forever."

The songs were mostly from the seventies and the eighties, a common thing at many clubs in Australia. That night, everyone sang along, during the most popular songs so loudly it drowned out the music.

Early on there was a dance-off; it was clearly highly competitive. One dancer was dressed in olive combat fatigues and wore a hat with a red star, the other looked like Wonder Woman in American red, white, and blue. The DJ cued up "Back in the USSR" and the two women squared off as the crowd made a circle around them, cheering. It looked like the Russian dancer in fatigues would lose, but at the last minute she tapped out. Her replacement dropped to the floor and went full airborne gator for fifteen feet. The crowd went wild. The Russians won.

The stamina was fantastic, the floor was always full, and everyone stayed in costume. It must have been difficult to dance for hours wearing a two-foot-high hat. At any given time, there were only one or two guys dancing; at last I could bring some value to our Australian enterprise. I stayed on the dance floor. Though my costume was slight, eventually I got overheated, so I grabbed some water and stood outside. At that moment "Be Faithful" by Fat Man Scoop came on and the DJ cranked up the volume. Praveen stepped outside and said, "John, this is your song," and held out his hand. I was being asked to dance. OK then.

I grabbed the offered hand, and Praveen led me onto the floor. This caused an outburst of enthusiasm. Boas were thrown. Things reached a sort of fever pitch, and I found myself dragging out the old moves of a young man. I am forever grateful that the video remains unposted. As Fatman was yelling, "Brooklyn Clan," I was in small town Australia, surrounded by dancing Elton John looka-likes. "Be Faithful" will always be a favorite, just the first notes take me back to that remarkable night with Ross and his merry band.

It was the last time I would feel unrestrained joy in my job.

PART IV
Final Chapter

Lessons learned:
Books matter, but only if everyone is free to speak through them.
Good intent matters; that is where kindness starts.
It is messy.

1.

Farewell

THERE IS A HOLTZBRINCK FAMILY LEGEND; I HAVE NO IDEA IF IT is true. When Georg von Holtzbrinck was dying, he made his daughter Monika promise that she would look after Fischer, Germany's most renowned literary publishing house, for as long as she lived. Whether the legend is true or not, from the day her father died in 1983 until the day she died in 2019, she watched over Fischer. She championed great books and had a deep commitment to preserving German literature, no matter what the cost. A multi-volume edition of the letters of Sigmund Freud does not bear monetary fruit, but at Fischer that mattered little. Monika was fierce in supporting the employees at Fischer, and she regularly encouraged them to enrich themselves culturally on company time. It was generally more about the books than the profits.

Monika and I knew each other in a boardroom sort of way until a complication arose within the Holtzbrinck family. At that point she asked me for some advice, and we grew closer. Some years later I was assigned the task of running Holtzbrinck's German publishing companies. Monika reported to me, at least on the organization chart. I reported to her brother Stefan, and owing to her position on the supervisory board, Stefan legally reported to her. All very German, and it made our relationship all the more complex.

Monika was shy and did not like confrontation. But when she felt strongly, usually about matters of principle, there was steel under her quiet manner. When we would disagree, usually about financial matters, we would push at each other. On rare occasions it would become tense, but we would invariably find a solution. There was always a gentle smile and kisses on both cheeks when we crossed paths. When things were difficult, she would occasionally ask for my guidance, and I for hers. We worked together for twenty-two years.

In the fall of 2019, Monika stepped down from the Holtzbrinck board. We had a supervisory board meeting a month or so later, my first one without her there in person or spirit. After the meeting was over, she came to the office to celebrate her eightieth birthday. It was a small affair, held in the open space on the third floor of the Stuttgart headquarters. The whole staff sang to her, not "Happy Birthday," but a popular song with lyrics specially sculpted for the event. It was an accomplished thing: someone played the electric piano, there was harmony, and for the chorus, they all sang her name.

After the last "Monika" was sung, the guest of honor stood behind a small high table with a vase on it. People came forward, one at a time, to wish her a happy birthday. Each carried a single rose and placed it in the vase. I waited until the end, and then walked forward slowly to place my rose. She took my arms in her hands, pulled me forward, and planted her usual two kisses.

I had heard a rumor that Monika was sick, but I was shocked to feel her cold skin. I mumbled something, probably Happy Birthday. Monika shifted me slightly aside; it felt like we were alone in a crowded room. She moved her hands from my arms to embrace my face, and she pulled my head close. Her eyes, just inches away, locked on mine. Her pupils expanded, and it seemed that I could see all the way into the back of them. I went completely still. She said only two words, she said them slowly, and she said them four times, "thank you . . . thank you . . . thank you . . . thank you." I faltered, then mustered a single thank you in return. Shaken, I walked away.

Monika left the room shortly thereafter; I didn't see her go. I was unsettled and mystified by the strange power of her eyes. I understood by the touch of her skin that she was very ill, and I wondered if that caused her odd intensity. Then suddenly it came to me: Monika was saying goodbye.

She died a few weeks later during the Frankfurt Book Fair. Stefan took the train back to Stuttgart to be with her in her last hours. He asked me to deliver his speech at the annual Holtzbrinck lunch for international publishers, scheduled for the next day. It was one of Monika's favorite events. His parting words were "You must prepare them for the bad news to come, but make sure they leave the room happy." It was a hard speech to give.

Monika gave me four thank-yous. I keep the fourth one, the extra one beyond the standard three. The others go to those who helped publish all the books she was so very proud of.

2.

Close Out

IN THE LATE SPRING OF 1981, I WAS FIRED ON A COLLECT CALL from a payphone in Billings, Montana. Thirty-nine years later, in the mid-pandemic summer of 2020, I was fired again. This time I was at my house in New York, and the call was incoming on an iPhone 8. I was standing outside a door, in the sun, just as I was in Billings. Stefan von Holtzbrinck, my boss, was on the line. He put it simply. "I have lost my faith and trust in you. We need to separate." I had known the call might be coming, but it was still a surprise, both in its content and in the words chosen.

In the early months of the pandemic that spring, Stefan worried constantly about liquidity. He felt the company was at serious risk if our sales declined significantly, and he was certain our sales would plummet. His views of the pandemic's effects were grounded in the German philosophical tradition of pessimism. My views reflected American optimism.

Stefan decided to make a series of changes that I disagreed with, including cutting salaries. After some robust objection, I agreed to implement the cuts. As time passed, our results kept improving, and by June they were much better than our original budget. I insisted that we immediately pay people back for the salary cuts we had put them through. Stefan wanted to wait and see what the future might bring. We clashed and, in a moment of conflict, I was impolite. The next day, after getting advice from someone in Germany, he agreed to pay people back immediately.

Several months later, on August 5, Stefan called and told me about a new plan he had devised to protect the capital structure of his family's holdings. I felt the plan was ill considered and unfair, but after telling him so, I agreed to carry it out. It was the owner's prerogative; my job was to get it done, no whining, no complaining. There was a deadline of four weeks to implement the plan, with a firm end date shortly thereafter to carry it out.

I set about the task with a small group of senior executives, all of us operating in secrecy. Two weeks later, after mountains of work and shortly before we needed to put the plan in motion, I thought hard about the effect it would have on our employees. I had been in frequent touch with them since the beginning of the pandemic and many had shared their distress: the murder of George Floyd and the protests that followed, parents stranded or dying alone, the struggle to make it through the day isolated in small apartments, the sirens, the fear. The problems were similar at all our offices and warehouses around the world. I knew with Stefan's new plan, hundreds would lose their jobs, and all would suffer an increase in their already overflowing anxiety. It was painful to imagine.

In a moment of clarity, I knew that we shouldn't do it, and that I wouldn't do it. The next day, August 21, I wrote Stefan a long email spelling out my arguments and pleading for a reversal of his decision. I reminded him that, despite the pandemic, our results were great and would only get better. I told him the employees deserved our deepest thanks, not this. I wrote with strong emotion. I also told him it was his choice if he wanted to go forward, but I would not help in any way. I hit "send" the next morning at 10:26 a.m.

Stefan responded, and he was not happy. He said he had discussed the matter with the Holtzbrinck board, and they had decided they could not go forward if I refused to help. They had scrapped the plan, both for the moment and for the future.

I thought the matter had been resolved, even though Stefan's voice carried a tight edge. I had refused to carry out a direct order. I had been impertinent. They were angry. But perhaps my arguments had been convincing. Perhaps they had agreed with me that, in its humanity, it was the right decision. Perhaps they had realized it was the best solution financially.

The next day, I got the gate.

I will never know the full story of why, but I suspect there was lots of complexity. These things are rarely simple. When it was announced several weeks later, I got lots of email. It was fantastic stuff; people in publishing really know how to write and they were all so kind. One such email came from an author I was fond of, Jim Comey. It had a postscript that offered useful advice, so I will share it, just in case you ever end up where I did: "PS: In similar experiences in my life, I found it helpful to occasionally whisper 'Fuck 'em' to myself."

I am no longer a publisher. My last day of work at Macmillan was December 7, 2020. I do not burn with anger, nor do I pine for days gone by. I am grateful for the time I had, and I will always remember the Holtzbrinck family well; they gave Macmillan remarkable autonomy, and they supported the causes we fought for.

But my last words about Macmillan are for the people of Macmillan. They will always have my enormous respect and admiration. They achieved all the goals they were given: They consistently grew faster than the industry, they made the Holtzbrinck family buckets of money, and they did less harm to the earth. I hope they all had a hell of a lot of fun doing it together. I sure did.

3.

Just a Cigarette
and a Gallop Away

M Y RELATIONSHIP WITH BOBBY GIBBS STARTED IN 1964, during a summer stay at his ranch. He was the first cowboy I ever knew. He died in January 1995, and I went home to Wyoming to be there when they put him in the ground. The Monday of the funeral dawned clear, with over a foot of new snow. The big event was scheduled for the early afternoon at the fairgrounds in Buffalo; Bobby never went to church and saw no reason to go at the end. As one of the speakers said later that day, "Bob was not a church-going man."

My mom and I were up early and decided to swing by her mountain cabin on the way into town. As we turned onto Crazy Woman Creek Road, I buckled up for the last four miles of rough track. There was no sign of a road, just snow. Mom gave advice: "The key to driving up here in this much snow is to never go under forty." True to her word, she never slowed down. It was an alarming drive, occasionally on the road but mostly off. Mom kept up a cheerful stream of chatter throughout. We made all three plank bridges at full speed and bounced off one large rock. We arrived mostly undamaged. Mom busied herself in the house, and I set out to say goodbye to Bobby.

I walked toward the mountains through the drifted snow and climbed a high ridge. I stood at the top, the sheer rock face of the Bighorns to the west, the Great Plains stretching to the east. It was cold and white, with only the sound of the wind for company. The creek ran through the valley below, and I imagined the water flowing out to the Powder River, where it would turn north toward Bobby's TY Ranch some ninety miles distant. I stood still. I thought about Bobby Gibbs, and what he had meant to me. In time, it felt like he was present, somehow still here.

Suddenly it was late morning and time to go. The roads in town were still mostly deep in snow, but all the routes to the fairgrounds had been plowed early. When we arrived, the parking lot was full. Inside the front door, on an easel, was a picture of Bobby. He was smoking one of his hand-rolled cigarettes and giving the guests that look he had: *Don't you have some work that needs doin'?*

It was crowded in the big central hall; most of the small town of Buffalo seemed to be there. People had driven in from seven states to say their final farewell and throw down some VO to ease their pain. Bobby wasn't big on music, but there was one old country singer he liked, and Mike Thomas was doing his best to cover those songs. The bartender was the law, in uniform, gun strapped to his waist.

Then the music stopped and the doors at the end of the room opened. Bobby came in on the shoulders of six pallbearers. They were evenly matched, gaunt and stringy, and they gimped down the aisle. He rested in a plain pine coffin that his three sons and his daughter had made the night before out at the ranch. They had branded it down both sides. TY. Wherever Bobby was going, they would know where he came from.

Dressed in their cowboy Sunday best, dark blue jeans, leather belts with rodeo buckles, and clean white shirts with pearl snaps, his kids followed the coffin They wore new black Stetsons with bald eagle feathers in the headbands. Thankfully the sheriff, on a break from pouring drinks, decided not to enforce the fine and jail time for possession of those feathers.

There were stories told that I no longer remember. Lots of them, and each one better than the last. No speeches, just stories, and his kids told the best ones. The tellers used Bobby's expressions, like "It's just a cigarette and a gallop away" or "If you can't sing 'Little Wrangler Joe,' you don't know shit." Some of the stories had names like "Best all-around cowboy" or "Beef, beans, biscuits, booze, and bullshit."

When the talking was done, they carried Bobby out the same way he came in. Six old cowboys shouldering the load, "Red River Valley" playing in the background, and not a dry eye in the house: "Remember the Red River Valley, and the cowboy who loved you so true."

Then the drinking started in earnest.

We buried Bobby in the cemetery on a hill overlooking the town where he was born, where he rodeoed, and where he died. They had managed to dig a hole in the frozen ground; Mom and I stood with Martha and the kids on the north side of the grave. The wind was blowing snow against our backs; I was huddled in goose down and Gore-Tex. Across the grave stood four leathered cowboys facing the wind, their legs bowed from lives spent on horseback. As Bobby was lowered into the ground, they stood motionless, their bare heads bowed, cowboy hats on their hearts. Three of the four had championship buckles, and though they wore nothing more than Levi's jeans and jackets, there was no sign that they were cold. The coffin came to rest, and they covered it with Bobby's old saddle blanket. Dust to dust.

I am now the same age as Bobby was when he died. It is hard to keep straight what was legend, and what was the man. He was part Indian, and he wore a spirit pouch around his neck his entire life. He grew up in the Bighorn Mountains, and the first time he came down to town he was eleven. He followed the often-quoted local wisdom, "I don't want to buy all the land, just the land that borders me," and he built a huge ranch over the decades. He hunted coyotes and eagles from his plane, he was a champion bareback bronc rider, and he got in bar fights from his teens to his late fifties. In his later years he would disappear into the mountains for weeks at a time, sleeping in a sheep wagon. Bobby didn't say much about any of it.

My memories of Bobby are small things, mostly faded. My first summer in Wyoming, when we lived briefly on his ranch, Bobby assigned me a big black horse named Nightmare. Early on we were out on a late afternoon ride and Nightmare took off on me. I remember trying to hold on desperately, finally sliding out of the saddle with the horse still at a full gallop. I landed hard in prickly pear cactus. Bobby helped me home, handed Mom a pair of pliers, and told her to put me in the tub first. As I grew up, every time I used pliers to pull porcupine quills out of a dog's nose, I remembered that bath at Bobby and Martha's house.

Years later, Bobby was there for a bad day at our place. My sister was unhappy as an early teenager; things were difficult at home. Reaching a breaking point that day, she ran away into the hills. When they eventually found her up in the high rocks, Bobby came to her alone, listened, and explained why she had no reason to feel badly about her actions, or herself.

A few years after that, on an early summer day, Bobby buzzed over our place in his Cessna, on his way home from Buffalo with groceries. He touched down in the hayfield behind our house and taxied up to the fence, dropping by for a cup of coffee. I was in seventh grade, trying out long hair for the first time. I ran out to meet Bobby as I always did. Any company is welcome when you live far from town, but Bobby dropping out of the sky was the best. He climbed down out of the plane and squared his hat on his head. He ducked through the barbed wire, gave me a hard look, and said, "Jesus, you look like a damn girl." And with that he reached into his pocket and snapped open his knife. I took off running for all I was worth, but slow young legs and sneakers were no match for his lightning reflexes in cowboy boots. He threw me down like a roped calf, put his knee in my back, and got to work with the knife. The barber in town finished the job the next day, and I went back to crew cuts for a while.

Time rolled by, and I would see Bobby once or twice a year. A few months before he died, I flew home to visit with him one last time. We sat in his living room; he had moved into town by then. He knew his time was short. We talked, more talk than was our custom. Finally, I asked Bobby if there was anything he regretted, or anything he still wanted to get done. He thought on it a minute, his face deadpan. Then he nodded slowly and said he did have one regret, something left undone. I asked him what it was. His answer was hard, and violent. He got the shocked effect he was after from me. I had to look him straight in the eye to see the laughter there. When I found it, his lip hitched up just a bit on the right side. He was dying, but he would be Bobby Gibbs to the end.

Twenty-six years later, and just a few months after my career in publishing ended, my mom died. We spread her ashes on a high hill at the ranch, along with the ashes of seven of her dogs that we found in a closet. In the distance you could see the rock face that towers over the high ridge on Crazy Woman Creek. A month after we scattered Mom, I went back to that ridge, as I do sometimes. I stood alone in the settled light of a summer evening. I thought of Neltje who had brought me here, and of Matthew and his small monument of ancient rock in the mountains. I thought of the vast empty land around me and I thought about Bobby Gibbs. He was more than just a cigarette and a gallop away, but even now, he lingered.

Epilogue

I T IS STILL DARK. THE EARLY MORNING NOISES HAVE BEGUN, though, and there is no need to look at my watch. The tile floor is hard, and I walk mostly on my heels to the bathroom. Then it is down the narrow steps, one at a time, my left foot always first. My feet do not work well anymore.

The trailer park is asleep. A few of the RVs have lights strung in the trees, still plugged in from the night before. A stray dog joins me as I reach the beach. Meager white ribbons rise from the dark water. It is still flat.

My son Jack and I have come to Mexico for forty-seven hours. We are here in the once small fishing village of Sayulita. Jack has moved to California from New York, but we have both been watching the same swell reports every day for weeks. We are here to be together in Mexico and to see some friends down the beach. We are here for the tropical warmth of the air and sea, and we have solemnly sworn to eat all our food wrapped in tortillas.

But really, we are here for the waves.

We arrived yesterday afternoon. In our desperation to surf, we paddled out into shin-high wavelets that were breaking over rocks in a foot of water. A long trip for a short wave. We consoled ourselves with dinner at a beach bar, and Jack legally ordered a beer for the first time, a Pacifico. We ate burritos and assured ourselves that tomorrow would be better.

But tomorrow has arrived without waves, and as our only full day in Mexico dawns, I sit on the beach and try to control my disappointment. But maybe we are in the wrong place. This beach faces north. There is a surf break somewhere nearby that faces south. And maybe there will be waves. We're going to find out.

Jack moves from horizontal to vertical fluidly. It is only a minute from asleep to out the door. Personal hygiene bores him and a swimsuit alone serves for clothes. We load the boards and set out. I have directions from a guy we met on the beach. Head back out of town and take a strange right before you reach the main road. Keep going until you reach the other coast and somewhere near the gas station, turn right again. Fortified with this rich local wisdom, we ease down the still-quiet streets, take the strange right, and head for the rugged hills. "Dad, do you know where we are going?" Of course I do. Winding through the dense forest, we make our way up one side of the escarpment and down the other. There are people and animals on the road occasionally. I am diligently alert, but the primitive unsigned speed bumps constantly avoid my detection. Jack takes to yelling "speed bump." He does not appreciate my superb driving skills.

Suddenly, the road dead ends in the jungle. We can go left or right, but this was clearly not featured in our directions. I am sure that it is better to go right. But as the minutes go by it becomes clear that our chance of finding any beach is remote at best. There is nothing but jungle and the occasional shout of "speed bump." Maybe it would have been better to go left.

Then a tin shack appears. There are no doors or windows, and chickens peck the dirt by the road. A small white pickup truck stands out front. The truck is badly battered, but there is a surfboard sticking out of the back. The driver is walking to the door as we take a U-turn and pull up beside him. He is stocky, rugged, and unsmiling. "Hola!" I say cheerfully. "Do you know where we can find some surf?"

He looks away glumly, then stares straight into the car and says with a heavy accent, "Are you good?"

I answer, "He is; I'm not very good."

This gets me a serious glare. "Beginners?" I say no. Another glare. "How good?"

I say, "Good enough, I think."

He stares at the ground for a while, then finally sighs, looks up, and says, "Follow me."

Without a hint of a smile he turns, gets in his truck, and drives away. Jack and I glance at each other and fall in behind. We drive for miles with no sign of the ocean. After a while I begin to wonder if this is a good idea. Jack says, "Hey Dad, do you think this is a good idea?" Of course it is.

Suddenly we turn right into the dilapidated entrance of a hotel. The road is crumbling at the edges. And as we approach a curve, I see a group of men and vehicles through the trees. I am getting ready to slam the car into reverse, when the white pickup suddenly swerves sharply left and bounces off into the jungle. I follow. We're on a dirt track that runs along an old, ragged fence. Tree branches scrape our windshield. Jack inquires again, "You sure this is a good idea?" I give Jack a grunt and try to plan what I will do if things go badly.

Then the track widens and there are two parked cars. The pickup stops and the driver gets out, peeling off his shirt as he turns toward us. He is short, but his chest and shoulders are massive. He is still glaring when he reaches us, but then his face breaks into a huge grin. We chat for a few minutes, and he tells us he is Brazilian, but his daughter goes to Dartmouth. Later, in the water, he will laugh and tell us that she has to tell all her high-powered friends that her father smokes dope and surfs all day.

As we unload our boards, he asks, "No wetsuits? Shit, this water is cold. I show you the way. Over here, the trail. Over there too, but too steep." As we climb down, the thin trail widens into a dry stream bed. "Fucking crazy getting down here in the rain. Fucking nuts!" The stream bed winds between huge ferns; vines hang from the trees. It is deep shade, but above us the canopy is bright green, and there are slivers of cloudless blue sky. "You see this fence? Private property now. I helped tear this fence down. Can't put a fucking fence between us and the waves."

Now there is more light in our green tunnel, and after a few more strides, we spill onto a bright white curve of empty sand. There is a cliff face rising from the beach on the right, and to the left the Pacific stretches to a distant range of hills. And there, right there in front of us, are large, perfectly peeling waves.

I gape for a second. Eloquently I describe my sense of wonder to Jack: "Holy shit!" Normally we might be high fiving or chest bumping, but now we rush straight to the water.

Our new friend says, "Go slow. Look, you must go in over here." We turn and walk down the beach while Jack reads the water.

He points and says, "Straight out here and then angle to the left to catch the current, right?"

This gets him a nod and a big smile. Then the smile disappears, and our man gets gravely serious. "It is big danger right here," he says pointing at the water, "rocks and fucking sea urchins. Fucking sea urchins. Fucking sea urchins will fuck you up." And then with a growl, "They will fuck you up no matter who you are."

Jack and I are charging now. Paddling out and giddy.

"Fucking sea urchins!"

"Did you check out the size of that guy's shoulders?"

"Damn, I thought we were done for back there!"

"Can you believe this?"

"How cool was that trail?"

"Look at those waves!"

There are six surfers at the break when we arrive. The sea has gone completely flat, and we wait together silently. There is no wind. The water is completely calm and clear; we can see our feet and the bottom below. And then the waves arrive, large mounds, seemingly from nowhere.

I watch from behind as Jack paddles into his first wave. The last thing I see are his feet giving that little kick as he begins to stand. And now here is a wave for me. I paddle. The wave takes the board, and I painlessly spring to my feet. The board drops down the face of the wave, and I carve to the right at the bottom. The water is smooth, blue under my board and green in front of me. The morning sun slants down the wave, lighting it from behind. In awe, I look down this sleek hump of the Pacific, more glass than liquid. And there, making his return trip in the warm morning light, is my son. He is watching me. I see his shaggy mop and his newly strong arms. I see his lazy smile and bright white teeth. He covers almost the entire length of his board, languid and relaxed, his feet slightly crossed. His back is arched, and he rests motionless on his elbows.

Jack is eighteen.

And this morning, in Sayulita, so am I.